M000083960

FASHIONABLE

DANCER'S CASKET

H.SEBALD

FRONTISPIECE.

THE

FASHIONABLE

DANCER'S CASKET

OR THE

BALL-ROOM INSTRUCTOR.

A NEW AND SPLENDID WORK ON

DANCING,

Etiquette, Deportment, and the Toilet,

BY CHARLES DURANG.

~~~~~~~~~
FOURTEEN BEAUTIFUL ILLUSTRATIONS
~~~~~~~~~

APPLEWOOD BOOKS
BEDFORD, MASSACHUSETTS

The Fashionable Dancer's Casket was first published in 1856 by Fisher & Brother.

ISBN 1-55709-444-6

Thank you for purchasing an Applewood Book. Applewood reprints America's lively classics—books from the past that are still of interest to modern readers. For a free copy of our current catalog, write to: Applewood Books, P.O. Box 365, Bedford, MA 01730.

Printed in the United States of America.

10 9 8 7 6 5 4 3 2

Library of Congress Cataloging-in-Publication Data
Durang, Charles.
    The fashionable dancer's casket, or, The ball-room instructor: a new and splendid work on dancing, etiquette, deportment, and the toilet / by Charles Durang.
         p.   cm.
    Originally published: Philadelphia: Fisher & Brother, 1856.
    ISBN 1-55709-444-6
    1. Dance.   I. Title
GV1751.D94   1996
793.33–dc20   96-28995
                                  CIP

DEDICATION.

To Francis Troubat, Esq., and Dr. Raymond Troubat.

GENTLEMEN :

Allow the author and compiler of this little terpsichorean volume, (matter selected from the best foreign authorities, and combined with indigenious composition,) to inscribe it to you, as a reward of your worth and good taste. As a tribute, not only to your zealous unrewarded services, in endeavoring to transplant to our *Soirees Dansantes*, the dancing novelties of the polished European circles ; but, as a profound sense of gratitude for many favors professionally and personally conferred.

I am gentlemen,
Your obedient servant,

CHARLES DURANG.

PREFACE.

The major part of these dances are danced in our assemblies and private parties, with many that are of foreign origin. The programme being selected and compiled, with choregraphic descriptions of the steps and figures, from the celebrated teachers of Paris and London, viz. :—Cellarius, Markowski, Coulon's and Mrs. Henderson, to which is added that lady's admirable treatise on Etiquette, Deportment and the Toilet.

vii

CONTENTS.

BADEN POLKA.

ETIQUETTE,

OR THE

Preliminary Instruction to Dancing.

THE TOILET.

THE first thing for a lady to consider, is simplicity of attire, whether the material be cheap or costly—such simplicity as produces the finest effect with the least apparent labor and the smallest number of articles.

The next thing to be considered is elegance of make and propriety of colors. Fashion in general will determine the former; but the latter must be left to individual taste.

In the selection of colors a lady must consider her figure and her complexion. If slender and sylph-like, white or very light colors are generally supposed to be suitable ; but if inclined to *embonpoint*, they should be avoided, as they have the reputation of apparently adding to the bulk of the wearer.

Pale colors, such as pink, salmon, light blue, maize, apple green, and white are most in vogue among the blondes, as being thought to harmonize with their complexions. Brilliant colors are more generally selected by the brunettes, for a similar reason.

Harmony of dress involves the idea of contrast. A pale girl looks more wan, and a brunette looks less dark, contrasted with strong colors. But as the blonde and the brunett are both beautiful in themselves, when the contour of the countenance and figure is good, a beautiful young girl, blonde or brunette, may without fear adopt either style, or both, for a change ; for a uniform mode of dressing, assumes at last the character of mannerism and formality—a character which is incompatible with the highest excellence in any of the fine arts.

The material of the dress should be of the lightest description—the more gossamere-like the better.

A rich satin slip should always have either crape or net over it ; and it is the generally received opinion, that the less trimming the dress has the better. On this point, however, individual taste may sometimes successfully make a deviation from the general rule.

Ladies, also, should remember that gentlemen look more to the effect of dress, in setting off the figure and countenance of a lady, than its *cost.* Very few gentlemen have any idea of the value of ladies' dresses. This is a subject for female criticism. Beauty of person and elegance of manners in woman will always command more admiration from the opposite sex than beauty, elegance, or the various fashionable costumes of the day.

It is the fashion at present to wear long dresses ; but in having the dresses thus made, orders should be given not to have them so long as to touch the ground ; for in that case they are apt to be torn before half the evening is over. It is almost impossible to thread the mazes of the dance without such an accident, if the dress should sweep the floor, except with a careful and accomplished cavalier.

The head-dress should be in unison with the robe, though ladies who have a profusion of beautiful hair require little or no artificial ornament ; a simple flower is all that is necessary. To those who are less gifted in this respect wreaths are generally thought becoming.

Tall ladies should avoid wearing anything

across the head, as that adds to the apparent height. A "chaplet" or a " drooping wreath" would, therefore, be preferable. White satin shoes are worn with light colored dresses ; and black or bronze with dark ones. The gloves should fit to a nicety.

Mourning in any stage—full mourning or half mourning—has always a sombre appearance, and is, therefore, unbecoming in a ballroom ; but since the custom of decorating it with scarlet has come into vogue, an air of cheerfulness has been imparted to its melancholy appearance.

A black satin dress looks best when covered, with net, tarlatan, or crape—the latter only to be worn in mourning.

Gentlemen's ball attire varies but little, as they generally appear in black. This is a thing *ad libitum*. The black neckerchief at present prevails ; with this the white waistcoat contrasts best, and is generally adopted. But when white or *fancy* neckerchiefs are worn, black or dark waistcoats prevail. Enamelled or patent leather boots are appropriate. Shoes, or pumps, have gone out, excepting at State balls, where court dresses are worn. White or lemon-colored gloves and embroidered shirts are fashionable.

THE BALL ROOM.

Ball-rooms, with their decorations, *ante-rooms*, etc., etc., like tastes, vary so much, that it is impossible to describe the particular form that prevails. But that which gives the greatest satisfaction has a form nearly square, one side being only a little longer than the other. The advantage of the nearly square form lies in this : that it may be used either for one or two quadrille parties, and one or two circles for the round dances, as circumstances may require ; whereas, were it perfectly square, it could not well be divided for two parties ; and were it very long, it could only be used at one end by a single party.

The top of the ball-room is that end of the room where would be the head of the table, were the room converted into a dining-room. It is generally farthest from the door ; but in cases where the orchestra is at one end, the orchestra end is the top, and will be found in general farthest from the principal entrance. It is always of importance to know and remember the top of the ball room, as ladies and couples at the top always take the lead in the dance.

Good flooring is indispensably necessary for a ball-room ; but when the floor is rough, the evil may be remedied by covering it with holland, tightly stretched. The practice in private houses—the holland may be drawn over the carpets. In public rooms, the size of the quadrillles is, respectively portioned out, in white paint or chalk. The room ought to be well lighted and amply ventilated—points not much attended to. Good music should be provided ; for bad music will spoil the best dancing, and destroy both the beauty and the pleasure of the entertainment.

When a lady and gentlemen enter a private ball-room, their first care should be to find their hostess, and make their obeisance. But on entering a public ball-room the gentleman takes the lady to a seat, or, waits at the lady's entrance, to conduct her to one. The gentleman should be gloved and in every way adjusted, before he enters the room.

When a gentleman goes *alone* to a ball (a general *habit* with our young gentlemen,) he should make application to the master of the ceremonies, or one of the floor managers, who will introduce him to any lady that he wishes to dance with ; and a gentleman so introduced will never be refused by the lady, if she be not already engaged, or form one of a party which she cannot leave ; for a refusal would be a breach of the law of good manners, as the master of the ceremonies is entitled and expected to be very scrupulous upon this point, and careful not to introduce to a lady any gentleman who is not *au fait* in dancing, or who is in other respects exceptionable. But no gentleman who is unqualified should seek an introduction under such circumstances. At a private ball the necessary introduction is made by the lady or gentleman of the house, or by a member of the family.

As ladies are not entitled to the privilege of asking gentlemen to dance, it is the duty of gentlemen to see that ladies shall not sit long waiting for partners, as it is one of the greatest breaches of good manners, that a gentleman can be guilty of in the ball-room, to stand idling whilst ladies are waiting to be asked. He has the appearance of one who is either peevish at a refusal, or too proud and contemptuous to dance with any but his *own* favorites.

Whatever preference may be felt, none should be shown in a public assembly of pleasure, which should be one large family, and universal urbanity should prevail throughout. Perfect politeness conceals preferences, and makes itself generally agreeable. Favoritism is only suitable for private life. Lovers are apt to forget this in the ball-room, and make themselves disagreeable, and sometimes particularly offensive, by their exclusive devotion

to one another.   The ball-room is not the
proper place for making love, but for general
and agreeable association.

Ladies especially ought to remember this,
as no lady, however beautiful, accomplished,
dignified, or opulent, can afford to lose the
good opinion of the society in which she
moves.   Moreover, beauty without good manners speedily creates feelings very different
from those of love.

A gentleman should not dance frequently
with one lady, nor engage a lady too many
dances in advance, as it obliges her to dance
more than may be agreeable to her; or perhaps
to forego the pleasure of dancing with a particular friend who may afterwards invite her.
A lady once refused to engage with a gentleman upon the plea that she was already engaged.   The gentleman requested permission.
to look at her programme, and, finding it not
filled up, presumed to write his own name
down for a late dance.   The lady replied,
"you may put your name down, but I shall
be at home when the dance is called."

If a gentleman should ask a lady to dance,
and receive a polite refusal, let him not exhibit any symptoms of dissatisfaction if he
see her dancing with another ; but he is certainly justified in never afterwards repeating
the request.

Never form an engagement during a dance,

Invitation and Bow.

or while the lady is engaged with another; never whisper to a lady, nor lounge about on chairs or sofas while the dance is proceeding.

Avoid all unfriendly or ungenerous criticism, ridicule, or satire, as such can never commend you to those whom you address, and may be repeated to your own prejudice. Besides they are out of harmony with the spirit of the ball, which is, or ought to be, an assemblage of kind and generous hearts, for soothing rather than for irritating the feelings.

In small parties, where there may be no programmes, engagements should not be made until the dance is announced.

Married couples ought not to dance with each other: there is, perhaps, no positive impropriety in it, and deviations from the rule may sometimes be either expedient or unavoidable; but it is more generous, and therefore more polite, for wedded gentlemen to dance with other ladies.

Balls should never be inconveniently crowded as this destroys both the beauty and the pleasure of the dancing. What pleasure can be derived in dancing a Quadrille or Waltzing, where you have not five feet square, to turn in? None truly. Charity balls, form an exception to this rule.

When the dance is over, the gentleman should invite the lady to take some refreshments.   Should she not accept of it, then he re-conducts her to her seat, and, unless he chooses to sit beside her, bows and with-draws.

In retiring from a private ball, it is not necessary to say "good night" to the host or hostess—when people are seen retiring it very often breaks up the party.   A quiet opportunity, however, should be sought of intimating your intention to leave, as it is more respectable and agreeable.

If there be a supper, the gentleman should conduct his *last* partner to the supper-room, unless he has a previous engagement to that effect, or is asked by the hostess to escort any lady she may desire.   In the last case he must provide a substitute for himself to his partner, making at the same time a suitable apology.

If a gentleman be introduced to a lady at a ball, he is not thereby entitled to claim her acquaintanceship afterwards.   He must not therefore bow to her if he meet her in the street, unless she do so first.

Abroad, the gentleman is entitled to bow to the lady afterwards.   But this is contrary to etiquette in polished society.

No gentleman should offer his services to conduct a lady home, without being acquainted with her, or requested so to do by the host or hostess.

Those who indulge in the pleasures of the

dancing *soiree*, should attend as early as possible, as their absence often detains its opening and continues the dancing to a late hour—one of the evils of public and private balls. In accepting the invitation to a private party, the hour of attendance should be adhered to as nearly as it can be—as those who are punctual feel uncomfortable until the other guests arrive. Besides, it looks as if you wished to appear of great importance, when you make your *entree* at a late hour.

QUADRILLE.

The Quadrille of all the fashionable dances, still retains the possession of the ball-room. The young and the old ever delight to walk or "trip it lightly" through the *old* Cotillion. It is not only the most social, as it admits of agreeable conversation and exchange of partners, but it is also the most simple, natural, and elegant in its movements, and the various figures into which it successively transforms itself. The variety of figures is *now* totally neglected.

The Quadrille, is adapted to all ages; the stout and the slender, the light and the ponderous, may mingle in its easy and pleasant evolutions with mutual satisfaction. Even a slight mistake committed by the unskillful in this dance, will not incommode a partner, or interrupt the progress of the movement; for each individual moves unrestrained, without the performance of the same step, (as in the waltz) and thus obliged to dance *ill* or *well* in the arms of a novice in the art.

Those who aim at aristocratic notions, or, who consider it beneath their dignity to dance

The Dancers in Repose.

25

or *gallop*, or for the sake of the elderly who
are incapable of dancing either, the habit of
walking Quadrilles with a sliding step has
now been universally adopted. Even the
lively gliding *chassé* promenade is very generally discarded in France and amongst the
higher circles in England, and with our best
dancing society ; nothing more than the correct musical steps, the graceful walk, and the
elegant demeanor, with a thorough knowledge
of the figure, is deemed requisite for taking
part successfully in a fashionable Quadrille.

Simple as this may seem in description ; it
cannot be gained but through the capable instructor's tuition ; dancing books may assist
the pupil's progress, but the style—or *walk*,
with the figures requires practice in classes.

The object of this refining art seems to be
lost sight of in the exaggeration of the present style of Waltzing, blending the ludicrous
with the indecorous, without the apology of
the received terpsichorean graces. From this
vitiated taste, it is in vain for the well-bred
teacher to indicate with precision and true
judgment the rules and character of the art—
to impart its original and graceful purpose to
the pupil—his suggestions and system are not
respected—but the surprise must cease, when
the sole direction of the social circle, is too
often left to the impulses of youth. Age,
which should preside at these amusements,

withhold their directing influence by absence, where their presence would command propriety of demeanor.

A Quadrille always consists of five parts—there can be no particular reason for this rule—but custom, which ever exacts its sway. In our ball-rooms, the figures of the Cotillion are few, viz. :—" Forward two"—" Right and left"—" Ladies chain"—" Swing corners"—and " Promenade all." These, are nearly all that are done, and with much annoyance to the dancer, called out at every eight bars, by the leader of the Orchestra. It is a vile custom, marring the melody of the airs—the teachers have nothing to do with their arrangement ; they may be practiced in their academies, but seldom taught. This matter as to the music and figures, is left to the fancy of the Orchestra. Those who aspire to the name of dancers, deem the plain Cotillion beneath them—while those who make no pretension to the art, conceive themselves quite adequate to walk, or, shuffle through them. The square form of the Cotillion is no longer practised in Europe ; That is, the side couples are thrown into parallel lines with the leading ones, and are thus formed up and down the room. In this way all the figures that are danced, can be easily executed ; with the exception of a few of the *good*, but now unfashionable old ones—viz. :—" New Year's

Day"—"Sociable"—"Coquette"—"Courtesy"
&c. Besides the alteration of this manner of
forming the Quadrille, will obviate the useless
and *ill-bred* contention which occurs for the
leading position. Couples should try to have
friends, or, some acquaintance with their *Vis-
à-Vis*, as this admits of that social interchange
which is so indispensable to keep up the spirit
of the dance.

However, as it will frequently appear that a
gentleman must dance *Vis-à-Vis* to a lady with
whom he is not at all acquainted, he must not
expect the lady to treat him, as a friend, with
pleasant smiles, or even with looks directed
towards him ; for the etiquette of society is
somewhat too scrupulous to admit of this fa-
miliarity. This prevailing etiquette is in direct opposition to the spirit of the dance, which
is that of sociality and interchange of kind
feelings. Many persons, however, exhibit extreme lack of taste and ill manners, in treat-
ing even friends and acquaintances with
averted looks, assuming pompous airs and
indifferent expression—a sort of *négligé* style,
which seems to say, " It is purely a matter of
condescension on my part to dance." It is no
compliment to a partner, or a *Vis-à-Vis*, to
assume such airs. It is, therefore, a style of
dancing unbecoming a lady or a gentleman.
All the fine arts must have the soul engaged

in them, to be practised in such a manner as
to command admiration.

It was formerly the custom for partners to
bow to each other on beginning a Quadrille.
This custom is discontinued, and the bow is
confined to the conclusion of the dance.

This is *now*, the foreign fashion—we should
like to see the *old* fashion kept.

The lady stands on the gentleman's right
hand in all dances.

The music of a Quadrille consists of eight
bars to a part; each bar corresponds to two
steps in the time, in walking the figure; and
the movements all consist of either eight steps
or four.

The first set of the London Quadrilles is
thus arranged—as they nearly conform to our
style and figures, it has been thought proper
to place them in our ball-room assistant.

FIGURE ONE.

1. *Le Pantalon.*

Top and bottom couples cross over (traversez,) eight walking steps—re-cross (re-traversez,) the same. This crossing and re-crossing is called *chaine Anglaise.* It is also called
right and left, and occupies eight bars. The
gentleman in crossing and re-crossing, always
keeps to the right of his *Vis-à-Vis* lady, keeping her inside the figure; in other words, he
moves first towards his own left hand, and
then towards his right, thus describing an arc,
or part of a circle—set to partners, that is,
chassé (move) four steps to the right, and four
to the left, turn partners (Tour des mains)—
ladies' chain—half promenade; *i. e.*, couples
crossing over to each other's places, hands
joined (Four bars, or eight walking steps)—
return apart to places (Four bars.) Side couples do the same—*if standing as in the old
method.*

2. *L' Ete.*

First or top lady or ladies, and opposite gentlemen, advance four steps—retire four steps
or two bars—move (*chassé*) four steps to right

and four to left, cross over, turning round at midway so as to be *Vis-a-Vis* to each other—eight steps in all—*chasse* to right and left, four steps each way—return towards partners, setting four to right and four to left—turn partners. Second lady and first gentleman repeat this—then side couples follow, the couples on the right of the top couple having the precedence. The lady on the right side advances to meet the opposite gentlemen.

3. *La Poule.*

First lady and opposite gentleman cross over, giving right hands—re-cross, giving left hands, and fall in a line—set four in a line, (in Philadelphia the four dancers set in a circle,) half promenade to opposite places—first lady and *Vis-à-Vis* advance and retire twice. (It used to be customary, in advancing and retiring, for *Vis-à-Vis* to bow to each other. This mark of courtesy is now discarded.) Both couples advance and retire, hands joined—return, half right and left to places—second lady and opposite gentleman repeat this—then the sides follow in succession.

Note.

The following remarks apply with equal force to our balls, as well as to the English ones.

In dancing Quadrilles, a very negligent and

disrespectful habit prevails of talking *loudly*
to partners, and setting with averted countenance to *Vis-à-Vis.* This is altogether out of
harmony with the spirit of dancing, and often
gives great offence to sensitive minds. If a
lady be not personally acquainted with her
Vis-à-Vis, she ought to give at least a modest
inclination of her countenance towards him,
and let her not forget a smile to a friend on
such an occasion.

4. *Trenise.*

The first couple or couples advance and retire, then advance again, the lady remaining
with the opposite gentleman. The gentleman
retires alone— the two ladies then cross over,
and he advances between them, turning round
at mid-way to be *Vis-à-Vis* to his partner—he
and his *Vis-à-Vis* lady then return to their
places—set to partners—turn round. The
second couple or couples then do the same ;
after that, the sides, or third and fourth couples, follow in succession. "This figure is
not often danced."

5. *La Pastorale.*

*This is the substitute for Trenise, to afford
variety : the two are never danced in the same
set.*

Leading couples advance and retire; advance again, the gentleman leaving the lady in the hand of the opposite gentleman, who advances and retires with both ladies, then advances again, and leaves the two ladies with the opposite gentleman, and retires alone. Opposite gentleman and two ladies advance and retire, then advance again, and join hands in a circle, (*tour des mains*,) going half round, and retire backwards in couples to opposite places ; and half right and left to their own places.   The second couples then take the lead in doing the same ; after that, the sides repeat the figure.

Note.

This is an alteration of our Cauliflower figure.   The *Solo of the gentleman being omitted in both ways.*

6. *Or Finale.*

Commences with *Le Grand Rond*—or Great Round : the whole party forming one circle, move four steps towards the centre, retire four steps, advance centreward four steps, again retire four steps.   After that, *L' Ete* is introduced, and *Le Grand Rond* is repeated after each figure.   In the joyous dancing circles, the *Finale* is made with a Gallop.   Couples, hands joined, advance and retire, hands joined with a Gallop step, cross over to opposite places, advance and retire again—re-cross to places. Ladies' Chain (*Chain des dames,*) half promenade to opposite places, return apart or half right and left.

Instead of the *Gallop* step it is common for the sedate and ceremonious dancer, to use the walking step. But the cheerful and the young, in all countries, use the *Gallop,* which is the popular style.

A good *Gallopade* round the room is a merry termination to the young—bow to partners—each gentleman then offers his arm to his lady, and conducts her to a seat.

COULON'S DOUBLE QUADRILLE.

INTRODUCED BY HIM AT LONDON, IN 1851.

Is danced by four couples, as the old Cotillion.   The figures being nearly the same—the
fifth one, being the Gallopade Quadrille known
to our ball-room dancers.

Figure 1.—Is the only *new* thing to our
dancers.

The top and bottom couples *Chaine Anglaise*,
or right and left, towards the centre, while the
two side couples dance *Grande Chaine* round
them.   All set and turn partners.   The four
ladies hands cross half round, seeing their
opposite gentlemen, and back again, swinging
their own partners into places, called the
Ladies' double Chain—the side couples repeat
the same.

It is thought proper to give with the foreign
dances the figures of the " Plain Cotillion,"
as danced with us, and as called out by the
ladies of the various ball-room Orchestras in
our city—this arrangement of figures has been
left *entirely* to their own direction, when it
most clearly belongs to the duties of the
teachers. There may be some variation among
the leaders, it is however, but slightly so.

PLAIN COTILLIONS.

AS DANCED IN PHILADELPHIA.

1st. *Figure*—Right and left
    2.—*Chassée* across—Lady to the *left*, gent to the *right* and set. *Chassée* back and set. This is the only time when a setting step is done.
    3.—Lady's Chain.
    4.—*Balancé*, or *double* promenade. (8 bars.) Sides repeat the same figure.

2d. *Figure*—Forward two—which means the top and bottom couples, advance up to each other and retire back again.
    2.—Cross over—*chassée* to right and left, and re-cross to places.
    3.—Balancé. Sides the same.

3d.—*Figure*—Right hand across.

Note.

This is the only call for this Cotillion. The figures that follow being understood. The figures of this Quadrille are repeated.

4th. Figure—Is sometimes the Cauliflower, *Sociable* and Courtsey Cotillions, or any novelty the leader may think of. If however, these are not played, the second Cotillion in the set is here repeated

5th. Figure—Right and left—Lady's Chain—Swing Corners—Promenade. "Sides the same."

Note.

All these figures can be danced in two lines, without the side couples.

The set sometimes finishes with the following *Gallopade Finale*.

Top and bottom couples *Gallop* quite round each other—*Same*, couples advance and retire, *same*, advance again, and change the ladies—Ladies' Chain—*same*, advance and retire—regain your partners to your places—Swing Corners—Gallopade all. Sides repeat.

In England the last Gallopade is extended at pleasure.

Note.

All these figures are danced in the measure of eight bars. The setting steps—*Balancés*—*Balloná*, etc., being done away with, also the *Dos-á-Dos*.

It were well for teachers, as for the true interests of the art, if the correct style of Cotillion dancing could be restored, as it would instruct young scholars to move with ease and grace. It is thus that *Cellarius* recommends the practice of the *Minuet de la Cour*, as a "study" to his pupils, which, although, a "dead letter" in the dancing assemblies, serves to impress on the form, positions both noble and graceful.

THE POLKA.

We have now to treat of a dance, that from the origin of a mere peasant step, has become the admiration of the fashionable world, at once exhilirating the dancers of the court and the rustics on the green.

The "Polka Valse" is the conqueror of all dancing—it has encircled its brow with the wreath of the Muse of the art; and, with this admission, think that, it has thrown the *graces* at the throne of ungracefulness; it certainly militates against the intention of its refinements.

Its rise and progress, as a simple dance, was truly remarkable, and marks the rapidity with which a fashion spreads over the world.

In 1843, this *Valse* made the grand tour of Europe; and soon gained a strong footing in America: so great was the excitement which it created, that its introduction into fashionable society may be regarded as the commencement of a new era in the art of dancing. The young, the old, and the middle-aged were roused by its attractions into a state that bordered on enthusiasm. Thus the sedate and the joyous—the learned and the unlearned—the professor and the mechanic, all were taken with its vivid and inspiring music and simple step, and followed its measures with enthusiasm--age and youth attended the dancing schools, or became lost in the Polka mazes of the ball room.

The love for dancing should never be repressed, through a too rigid morality, for while it brings the two sexes together in social communion, its graces, under proper tuition, impart a true taste for an elegance of deportment and a wish to please in the attributes of polished manners. It gives to the influence of woman to wean the male sex from those very gross habits of drinking, smoking, gambling, chewing and revelling, to which it is prone when left *undirected*; while it develops the inherent power of the female sex, when clothed with the polite accomplishments, to correct and reform from these revolting practices, restoring man to his original dignity and usefulness; which he repays by his chivalrous protection, attentions and agreeable society.

Much has been said about the origin of the Polka; that it is an ancient Scythian dance; known and practiced in the Northern countries of Europe: namely, Russia, Servia, Bohemia, Germany and Hungary.

All this may be true, but, we remember it
as an old Scotch step, since our boyhood.

There is only one Polka known or recog-
nized in the fashionable world; but the style
of dancing it varies considerably. The most
elegant people, and the best dancers, always
dance it in a quiet, easy style; and those gentlemen who rush and romp about, dragging
their partners along with them until they become red in the face and covered with the dew-
drops of a high corporeal temperature, are
both bad dancers, and men of very little good
breeding.

THE MANNER OF DANCING IT.

The gentleman should pass his right arm
round the lady's waist, (not too much so,)
holding her with sufficient firmness to be able
to take her through the mazes of the waltzers
with perfect safety. Her right hand should
be held in his left hand, which he should raise
towards his left shoulder in such a manner
that he may be able to turn her round as with
a lever, or point out as with an index the
movement which he contemplates. The lady
rests her left hand on the gentleman's right

shoulder, her head slightly inclined towards the left.

As the Polka is the fashionable ; nay, the universal dance of our society, we will take a lengthened notice of its elements and analytical construction by the first teachers in Paris and London ; to which we venture to offer, through a battery of foreign prejudice, our opinion and mode of teaching it.

We first select from the work of *Cellarius*, the principal teacher at Paris, who therein makes some very judicious remarks upon the waltzing attitude.

The position of the gentleman and lady, in dancing the Polka, is almost similar to that of the ordinary waltz. The gentleman should place himself opposite his lady ; he should support her with the right hand placed around the waist. The arm, destined to support the lady, alone requires a certain degree of vigor ; a natural grace, an elasticity, and an extreme ease, should prevail in all the movements of the gentleman.

The left hand, which holds the lady's right, should be half extended from the body ; the arm neither too *stiff* nor too much bent, which would look affected in one case, and *gauché* in the other.

The gentleman should hold his lady neither too near nor too distant from him : too great a proximity would be contrary to the laws of

propriety and grace; while too great a distance
would render very difficult, if not impossible,
the turns and evolutions which form a part
of this dance. In short, the gentleman must
determine, by his own good taste, the law of
that space which is to exist between his partner and himself.

The lady should place her right hand in
that of the gentleman's, the other gracefully
resting on his shoulder; she will leave her
head in its natural position, and avoid raising
it, lowering it, turning it to the right or left;
the most simple attitude being the best adapted to the Polka, as indeed it is to all dances
and Waltzes we are about to describe.

She should let herself be guided entirely by
the gentleman, who alone imparts to her the
direction of the dance, conducts her to this or
that part of the ball-room, and decides the
repose and the re-commencement of the dance.
A lady is reputed so much the better waltzer
(*if there is nothing indecent in the dance,*) as
she obeys with confidence and *ease* the evolutions as directed by the gentleman.

We quote the above *proper* remarks, from
Cellarius, as the great authority in these
things; in the hope that it may effect some
change in the indecent waltzing attitudes, prevailing in our dancing circles. The teachers
in Philadelphia, should at once check its im-
modest tendencies. As far as we can learn,

they all forbid its practice in their respective schools.

If the instructors of the art, have its *elevation* in view as a profession, they will refuse to permit vulgar positions and movements in the dances of society.

RULES AND STEPS OF THE POLKA.

There is no rule respecting the direction in which the Polka should be performed. This is left to the option of the person to decide. It may be danced to the right or to the left in turning, and backwards or forwards, likewise in turning; or, in cases where there is not sufficient space to proceed, the Polka step and position may be preserved in making a kind of a *Balancé* or set. Practice in all waltzing, is the only way to give ease and skill. In a room where four inferior couples would be limited for space, twenty good couples would waltz with great ease : above all, avoid elevated steps and forced action in all dances. *Quietness* and *neatness* without stiff *preciseness*, are the true characteristics of the lady and gentleman.

THE POLKA STEPS, AS TAUGHT BY E. COULON.

" There are only three steps in the Polka, which are all *jumped*, and occupy one bar of music, the fourth interval being only a repose to give time to prepare for the next foot.

To begin, the foot is raised a little behind, the gentleman using his left, the lady her right foot. The gentleman then, for the first step, springs lightly on the right foot, and almost simultaneously slides the left foot to the side, finishing on both feet, with the knees bent. For the second step he makes a *jeté* with the right foot which brings the left foot extended to the left, and raised a little from the ground ; for the third step he makes a *jeté* before with the left foot, and finishes with the right foot up, a little behind. Then, without stopping, he bends on the left foot, in order to employ the fourth interval of the bar, and proceeds in the same manner with the right foot. The lady does the same, only, as I have mentioned, beginning with her right foot.

"The musical rhythm of the Polka may be explained thus :"

Note.

This mode of teaching the step, leaves the pupil to make one *silent* count of a Quaver ; no easy task to explain to persons, without a musical ear or knowledge of any kind, to comprehend.

THE STEPS OF THE POLKA BY CELLARIUS.

The Polka is danced in *two-four-time*, a military march movement, rather slow.

I will endeavor to give our idea of the step, begging my readers to excuse what in this demonstration, as in all others of the same kind, must be necessarily a little tedious; for in this, more than ever, I must put aside all pretension to elegance of style, and endeavor only to attain *clearness* and *exactness*.

The step of the *Polka* is divided into three times.

For the first time, the left heel must be raised to the side of the right leg, without passing behind it, and so as to glide along the calf. In this position you spring upon the right foot, so as to throw the left foot forward, which forms a *glissade en avant*.

The second and third times are composed of two *jetés*, or *petits pas sautés:* the first with the right, and the second with the left foot; taking care that the two feet are kept nearly in the same line.

At the second *petit pas*, you lift the right leg, the heel near to the lower part of the left calf; and you let the fourth time of the measure form a pause or rest, so that three times only are marked by the dance. You re-commence with the *glissade en avant* of the right foot, and so continue alternately."

Again he says—" On the first introduction of the Polka, figures were executed. The gentleman led out his lady, holding her right hand, as in the old Hungarian dance, then turned towards her, and turned from her also alternately. With the ordinary step was mixed that called the *Bohémien* or Double Polka, which they executed with the left leg in the second position, the heel to the ground, the toes in the air, (*the heel and toe done here*) exactly as in the *pas de polichinelle* !"

Thus he descants on this step, in several pages. I took the liberty in our school, to suppress the "heel and toe," in the Polka Quadrilles, simply pointing the toe, as in better taste, (at least for the ladies,) and, we believe it has been generally adopted.

We now give the method of *Mrs. Henderson*, a popular teacher at London—who seems to be more *clear* on the subject, than any of her celebrated contemporaries.

The Polka step is very simple. It consists merely of three steps and one rest. The gentleman begins with a slight spring on his right foot, at the same time sliding the left foot forward. This is the first movement (the toe of the left foot being pointed outward, and the heel pointed toward the right foot.) The right foot is then brought up to where the left is, at the same time raising the left foot. This is the third movement. After a rest of one quaver, spring with the left foot, and slide the right forward, thus reversing the movement, and do as before with the opposite foot. As the lady begins with the right foot, springing on her left, the above directions apply to her.''

The Polka step, as thus described has been greatly modified with our dancers—its original characteristics, as on the hop and drawing up the foot along the calf of the leg, is not done.

Our *theory* of the step is thus—there are four beats in the Polka Bar, and, as a natural movement—(for all steps and motions in dancing must conform to nature, adjusted by art,) we have taught four beats in the step, and in this way it harmonizes with the music and the *old Scotch step* from which it is derived.

The gentleman in waltz position with his lady—(the toes about half inclined in,) begins with sliding his left foot sideways (counting 1,) then bring the right foot to the left one, [2,] again slide left foot, (a very small way,) [3,] and make a gentle hop on the left foot, for the fourth count—repeat this movement to the right, with the right foot—" Slide to right with right foot, [1,] bring up left foot to right foot, [2,] slide right foot again, (counting 3,) and keep on right foot, [4.]

Thus alternately from right to left—forward and backward—or, waltzing to right and left in turning.

The lady of course, using the reverse foot to her partner. The way it is generally executed with us is nothing more than a small *chassée*, ending each time with a rise upon the toe, or, a slight hop. It may be taught in a *trot* motion, as coming near the French expression of *jetés*—and, it is often done so. The French language abounds in laconic *apt* phrases to express steps and figures that the English one does not possess.

RULES TO BE OBSERVED IN WALTZING AND GALLOPADING.

In this age of waltzing, we need not dilate at length upon the general rules to be observed; but we consider it highly necessary parties should strictly adhere to the following hints. Either of the above are danced by an unlimited number of couples following each other in a circle.   Any couple, from fatigue or other motive, should be careful to retire to the centre of the circle, by which means confusion with the following couples is avoided.

The Polka requires considerable practice on the gentleman's part to dance it well ; for he, especially, has to guide the lady through the *mass* of confused waltzing couples into which it usually forms itself: and herein lies the skill of the gentleman waltzer, sustained by the easy dexterity of his partner—it is to preserve the step and time and perform the various evolutions in gracefully avoiding collisions with the other couples in whirling by them, or, in threading gently through the " *cretan labyrinth* " of the modern waltzing ball-room.

The present style of our dancing is truly sub-
versive of all refinement and the true purposes
of dancing. All romping, dragging, hugging
and leaning or stooping over the shoulders of
partners is decidedly objectionable, and only
fit for places of loose resort. In our respectable private houses, we hope that it will not
be allowed. It must be confessed, and, we
refer to it with regret, that our public balls,
even those of high pretensions, are very far
from being free of the indecorous objections
we mention above. Many of those who claim
intellectual superiority and assume the *glass*
of *fashion* set the example of these European
vulgarities, in dancing—dress—huge beards,
etc. John Bull, in this nonsense, imitates
his Continental neighbors, and, which, our
unsophisticated feeling servilely imitates—an
obsequiousness unworthy of American spirit.
Why can't we be original?

Fvery accomplishment is liable to be abused
—even those the most pure and intellectual,
and, so has the rustic Polka, which was a gay
and animated *Valse* on the village green, trans-
planted to the fashionable *Soirées dansantes*,
became infected with vulgarities. But a person of refined taste and a lover of moral deportment, can at once perceive the difference
between the elegant and the inelegant, the
delicate and the indelicate.

The cultivation of the arts is to improve the

taste and to elevate the feelings, and while
purely practised, they most beautifully accomplish these desired views ; all ages attest their
beneficent influences on mankind—but when
perverted to base purposes they corrupt. How
often have we seen painting—sculpture—
music and even poetry, made to laud and sus-
tain *evil*, when their heavenly attributes were
to cherish the virtues.   The benefits of nature
are daily abused—and, as it has been truly
said—" Gold itself, the most incorruptible of
metals, is the most corrupting of them all."

So let us protect dancing for its *uses*—not
condemn it for its *abuses.*

" The Polka thus consists of two opposite
linear movements, one towards the right, another towards the left.   At the same time, a
circular movement goes on which completes
one half of the circle in moving to one side,
and the other half in moving to the other side,
and a progressive movement at the same time
goes on in the orbit of the great circle.   The
step can also be executed moving forward in
a straight line—the one partner going forward,
while the other goes backwards, and *vice versa.*
The circular movement can be made either
from right to left, or from left to right, at
pleasure ; but it always begins with right to
left, so that the other is called the reverse
turn, but the step is precisely the same in
both.

Like the earth in its orbit, the Polka Valse consists of two circles, a great and small one. It turns on its axis while it revolves round its great centre of a circle—wheeling round in a small circle of eight steps each, or six steps and two rests, agreeably to the idea of the old notion of steps. Like all Valses it is *ad-libitum* in performance, in which much latitude is allowed. The great circle of the waltzers should be preserved in proper distances, and if so, the figure looks extremely well—but, in this preservation obstacles occur so rapidly from the impulsive progress of the revolving couples as to preclude anything like rule. The exigencies of the waltz are numerous, and that which seems to the mere observer *confusion worse confounded*, is but the order of the figure preserved in merry deviations, or the irregular freaks of the waltz to beautify its eccentric evolutions. The circle always commences with great perfection, each couple following the other in regular succession : but, it ever falls into most *admired confusion*, but it requires every gentleman to be thoroughly master of the steps and its various turnings. The reverse of all this, is mostly found, that is, the ladies are generally the better dancers. The waltz of all kinds, is often continued to a period of ten or, oftener fifteen minutes. In this lengthened space of time, much giddiness of the head must ensue, and does, at-

tended by fatigue and want of breath. The
circular movement finds ease and restoration,
in waltzing forward and backward in straight
lines—or, making a kind of *Balancé*, with the
same step. This retiring or advancing in a
right line, as the gentleman indicates, is known
to waltzers as the *redowa* pursuit—The skil-
ful director, when the crowd leaves to each
couple scarcely space to move—to *pivot* upon,
he slackens his steps so as to form a space for
himself. If the lady has no wish to quit the
floor—the gentleman may quietly waltz into
the centre of the circle, continuing with a
a *Balancé* Valse in place—when refreshed, she
can rejoin the circle. The step used in the
back or forward waltz—is only a *chassée*,
or gliding with the feet, without any hop—*pas
Marche* style.

Mrs. Henderson, a teacher of dancing, says:
" Ladies, however, not being all alike ; either
in figure or facility of movement, should consider well whether or not they are imposing a
severe task on their partners by their passi-
vity, and generously assist them when they
seem to require it. A lady who dances well
can easily do this, and however ponderous in
person, may make herself as light, in the arms
of a partner, as a slender girl of eighteen.

Many ladies of magnitude, however, object
to do this, and play the passive young girls,
and thus convert a light and agreeable pas-

time into a task of extreme toil and hardship
to the gentlemen who dance with them.

The gallantry of the gentleman seldom make
more of this than material for an innocent
joke; but even this may very easily be avoided
by a little more activity on the part of the
lady.   It is very well for slender young ladies
to be led ; but a woman of mature figure and
stately appearance aspires to lead, and the
leadership becomes her when dancing with
boys, even though the boys be *old ones.*"

Much of what is objectionable to a delicate
taste, perhaps, arises from bad dancing ; but
there are good dancers who yield themselves
up to the excitement of the moment, forget
the proprieties of social etiquette, and descend
into the vulgarities of low and irresponsible
society, that has no character to support.

THE VALSE.

Within the last few years the Valse, like many other human institutions, has undergone a complete revolution or reform. Notwithstanding, as in politics so in dancing, there are conservatives who prefer the *good* old system and regret its decline.

The old Valse (the word waltz has now gone out of fashion ; moreover, the Germans pronounce it Valse—the *v* for the *w*,) was a dance in three times, slow and stately, wheeling round in one direction only, and not susceptible of a reverse turn, or a forward and backward movement. The consequence was, that, notwithstanding the deliberation with which it was conducted, most people became giddy with the motion in a very few minutes. The Valse *à Deux Temps*, or two times, has introduced an important reform or revolution in this respect—for the step is of such a nature that it can be made in a rotary movement from right to left, or from left to right ; or it can be walked in a straight line backwards and forwards, thus enabling the parties to cor-

GERMAN VALSE:—

Or, Valse à Trois Temps.

rect the slightest tendency to giddiness, so soon as it is experienced.

In England the *Deux Temps*, is very much danced—and the chief cause for this preference is, no doubt, that it prevents the giddy sensation, one of the *disagreeables* of the incessant whirlings of the old waltz.

This Valse is not popular with us, although it was introduced at the time of the Polka—and, has been but coldly received everywhere, either as a dance by itself, or interspersed with the steps of other dances. But, as we said, it is much danced in the London fashionable circles.

The Polka mania was perhaps, indispensable to complete the revolution that has been effected ; and the Polka, being a dance which is susceptible of all the various movements above alluded to, and with all a dance which is easier of execution, and less giddy in its effects, was peculiarly fitted for preparing the way for the future triumph of the *new* over the *old* Valse. Once the Polka was learned, the fate of the old Valse was sealed.

The Polka and its kindred have been much indebted for their success to the soul inspiring music of the day—to the genius of Monsieur Jullien, Strauss, and other composers of brilliant talent. The new dances thus introduced, were received by the dancing public in Europe

and America, with the most enthusiastic feeling—whose inspirations at once overturned
the stately and decorous Quadrille.

The Polka and Mazurka music express the
time in so very clear and intelligible a manner without any sacrifice of melody or harmony, that the recreation of the dancing assembly has received a new impulse—a novel
charm almost irresistible in its nature.

Youth became inspired—and age realized
youth. The extraordinary result of the Polka
and its music !

STEP OF THE OLD WALTZ.

CALLED WITH US THE PLAIN ONE.

Valse à trois Temps.

This Waltz is still a favorite with us, but there is much difficulty with pupils in learning it—and, much diversity of opinion among the masters in teaching it. Many modes have been adopted to impart this Valse—many who have a talent for dancing acquire it, almost intuitively—others again may labor for years, and never get it.

We shall merely describe the gentleman's step, the lady's being precisely the same with the opposite feet—*i. e.*, right for left, and left for right—*à contre jambe.*

The gentleman should place himself directly opposite his lady, upright, but without stiffness ; joining hands, the left arm of the gentleman should be rounded with the right arm of the lady, so as to form an arc of a circle, supple and elastic.

The Step.

1st. Gentleman slides left foot diagonally backwards.

2d. Slide right foot past the left in the same direction, turning slightly to the right.

3d. Bring the left foot again behind the right.

4th. Slide the right forward, still slightly turning to the right.

5th. Slide left foot forward again.

6th. Turn on both feet, finishing with the right foot forward.

All turns are to the right for the gentleman, to the left for the lady.

———

We subjoin the Cellarius' method of teaching this waltz, as it may prove acceptable to all waltzers.

The gentleman sets off with the left foot, the lady with the right. The step of the gentleman is made by passing the left foot before his lady. So much for the first time.

He slides back the right foot, slightly crossed behind the left; the heel raised, the toe to the ground. So much for the second time.

Afterwards, he turns upon his two feet, on

the toes, so as to bring the right foot forward, in the common third position, he then puts the right foot out, on the side—slides the left foot on the side, in turning on the right foot, and then brings the right foot forward, in the third position. So much for the fourth, fifth, and sixth times.

The lady commences at the same moment as the gentleman, with the fourth time, executes the fifth and sixth, and continues with the first, second, and third ; and so on.

Before the first six steps are completed, they should accomplish an entire turn, and employ two measures of the time. Formerly, they counted by three equal steps ; this has been properly reformed, seeing that the three first steps are not made like the last. The last plan is to count by six steps, connected one to the other, in order to make the pupil feel the time he should mark. The foot of the lady, as well as that of the gentleman, should preserve its ordinary position ; all unnatural turns, or bending of the foot, can only spoil the waltz.

The lady should neither dance on her toes, nor with her heels as though they were nailed to the floor, the half of the foot only, should remain on the ground, so as to preserve the utmost solidity, without detracting from the lightness.

THE SCHOTTISCHE.

Of all the new dances which have been introduced within the last few years, none ap-
pears to be a more general favorite than the
Schottische Valse. It successfully contends
with the Polka for *Terpsichore's* ball-room
favors. But although it ranks in novelty and
fascination with the most attractive of the
new dances, and the learned in the art refer
its origin to antiquity, as they did that of the
Polka, yet, in truth, it is no more than a German peasant dance.

The music, too, is Germanic and of antiquity, although it impresses us with novelty
and inspiration. The Schottische is now as
universally danced as the Polka. being susceptible of all the evolutions pertaining to the
other circular dances. The steps of this Valse
have been, with us, successfully applied to
Quadrille figures.

The Schottische does not require so much
practice as many of the dances, and, when
properly executed, is a very elegant and with
all a pleasing movement, for it is a contribu-

SCHOTTISCHE BALANCÉ.

At the top of the Schottische Valse.

67

tion of two movements, a Polka *one* and a circular hop movement; and the two combined make up a most agreeable variety not to be found either in the Polka, the *Deux Temps*, or the Redowa.

The step is very easy, but the double movement requires so much more care and attention than the Polka, that it becomes more difficult for the gentleman to guide his partner through the mazes of the Schottische without encountering many of those awkward mishaps, such as treading upon toes and dresses, to which unskilful dancers are constantly subject through the agency of an invariable law of nature, which punishes learners in dancing as Schoolmasters punish pupils; only with a different instrument.   It is chiefly in the waltz —or circular hop movement that the difficulty is experienced; for if the time be not precisely kept, so as simultaneously to make the two hops, a collision is inevitable, an awkward pause immediately ensues, to the great discomfiture of both parties, but especially to the gentleman, on whom the chief responsibility lies.

It is perhaps important for the cultivation of the art of dancing, that the gentleman's part is really more difficult, and requires greater practice, whilst gentlemen in general devote less time and attention than ladies to the acquisition of the accomplishment.

THE STEP OF THE SCHOTTISCHE.

The gentleman holds the lady in the same
manner as in the Polka.   He commences with
the left foot, merely sliding it forward, (or
side ways,) count one.   Then he brings up
the right foot to the place of the left foot
(count two,) again sliding the left foot to the
left, (count three,) then gently hop on left
foot (4.)   He repeats this movement to the
right, beginning with the right foot, sliding
it sideways right, bringing up the left foot to
the place of the right, and sliding the right
foot sideways again, the hopping on the *same*
foot, count as before, (4.)

Immediately after the movement changes
into a series of double hops and double rotation.   Thus, spring on left foot. (count 1,)
hop on the same foot, (2.) turning half round;
spring on right foot, (1) hop on right foot (2,)
turning half round again—repeat the same
with left foot (2,) turning half round as before
—repeat the same with right foot, (2) turning half round—which will make eight beats

and two whole turns.   It is sometimes only
done with one whole turn.

Then begin the *balaneé* again, (the first step)
and circular step.

The lady' step is the counterpart of the
gentleman's, she beginning with the right
foot.

Note.

This Valse was somewhat modified by the
teachers in Europe, when first introduced,
from the plain German mode.   The first part,
termed the *Balancé*, was to advance and retire, instead of going right and left ; which,
was certainly much neater and more in the
nature of the art.   But this was thought to
create collisions, (the eye not being directed
backward) which it was always prudent to
guard against, for even good waltzers are liable to encounter them from the awkwardness
of the unskilful.   These collisions are far
less likely to occur in the right and left, or
diagonal, than in the forward or backward
movement.

The Schottische, like other circular dances,
may be varied by means of the reverse turn,
or even in going in a direct line round the
room.   The step rather changes in this figure
of retiring and moving forward to a *pas*

marché (or walking steps) gliding back like the *Redowa pursuit.*

The waltzers, may also double each part by giving four bars to the first part—and four bars to the second or circular movement.

The gentleman is expected to regulate all these matters, according to circumstances, sometimes for variety, sometimes to avoid collision in a crowded room ; and it is only necessary for him to apprise his partner of his intentions, by saying "double," or "four bars," and she repeats the sliding step instead of proceeding to the hop.

In England, they introduce the *Deux Temps* step into the circular part ; but this destroys the character of the Valse, and confounds two dances together.

The Schottische is easily acquired, unlike the *Deux Temps*, which requires only a few lessons to learn, but many to perfect it.

The time is nearly the same as the Polka, but often danced much slower. The Americans dance it faster than the Germans. This however is all a matter of feeling.

COULON'S EXPLANATION OF THE
SCOTTISCHE STEPS.

The gentleman begins with the left, and the lady with the right foot.

Three *pas Marche* (or walking steps) sideways, finishing with one foot up behind, then jump on the foot that is down. The same with the other foot.

Four times *jeté* forward, and jump on the foot which is down in turning one round ; this to be repeated four times. Lately the Valse *à Deux Temps* has been introduced instead of the four *jetés* and *jumps*—it is far superior.

Some begin the Schottische with four steps of the Gallopade, and then four *jetés* and

THE POLKA MAZOURKA.

The Polka Mazourka is a waltz danced by two. It is in great favor in our *Soirees dansantes.*

Explanation.

The gentleman begins with the left, the lady with the right foot.

This waltz is composed of two steps of the Polka with this difference, that the last part of the first step is a *fouatte* behind (hop and pass the foot behind,) after which it is the second step of the Polka, with the same foot as the first step.

The first step is taken sideways, and the second in turning half round. The position is the same as in the waltz.

POLKA.

Introduction before the Waltz Position.

THE REDOWA.

The Redowa is a Valse, the step of which has been taken from the second Mazourka Quadrille, which was first introduced into the fashionable world in Paris, and afterwards in London, by *Coulon* and *Mrs. N. Henderson*, at the Almack Rooms, in 1847, and whose instructions in the *Valses* and *Mazourkas* we have principally followed in our schools in Philadelphia. In the social dancing circles the *first* and *second* Mazourka Quadrilles presented insuperable difficulties in their execution. They were too complicated to acquire easily, and it was seldom that a sufficient number of persons could be found in a private party to make up the full number of eight, required, and possessing a thorough knowledge of the steps and the figures of the dance. It was therefore deemed advisable by the profession, to introduce the principal step in a valse or two, so that a small or greater number might dance it together, as circumstances permitted. This transformation of the dance greatly facilitated its reception into the private party; but, notwithstanding the beauty of the

step, the elegance of the movement, and the
pleasing character of the music, the Redowa
has not become a very general favorite. It is
frequently danced, but it must yield the precedence in popularity to the Polka, the Schottische, etc.

There is really no accounting for public
taste in dancing, and we think that the ease
and elegance of deportment is much sacrificed
in the statue-like position in which our ball-
room dancers move in steps and figures. We
make but a simple remark, not wishing to
trespass upon the opinions of teachers, or to
intrude our own ideas as regards rules of grace,
upon the received public taste and its established customs. But we may be permitted
to say that, the most popular Valses are not
only vivid and animated, but they preserve
the body upright, and the spine almost im-
movable during their performance. The Redowa, however, requires a rising and falling
somewhat resembling the manner of a minuet,
and suggests an idea of better address and
greater ceremony than the more popular Valses.

There seems to be a prevailing tendency to
the simple, the cheerful, and the rapid, in
dancing, rather than to the elegant and graceful; for there can be little doubt that the
style of the slightly bending, in the *Cellarius*
and the *Redowa*, are more in accordance with

grace of motion, than those which have suc-
ceeded in captivating the affections of the
public.

The step is as follows, supposing the lady
to commence :—Stand in third position, (right
foot forward) spring on right foot, bringing it
up behind the left foot, at the same time raising left foot, (count one ;) slide left foot forward, slightly bending the knee, (count one ;)
bring right foot up to left, with a slight hop,
again raising left foot, still keeping it forward, (count one ;) spring on left foot, bringing it behind right, and raising right foot
with a slight hop, (count one ;) slide right
foot forward, bending knees, (count one ;)
bring left foot up to right, with a slight hop,
raising right, keeping it forward, (count one ;)
this is the forward movement ; the gentleman
merely reverses the feet.

For the circular movement, the lady slides
the left foot forward, and the right back. The
gentleman, *Vice Versà.*

The reverse turn may also be used in the
dance to form a variety. The step is almost
the same as the *pas de Basque* ; the only difference is the hop. This Valse is still quite
fashionable.

In dancing the Redowa, care should be
taken to mark well the first and third crotchet
in the bar, otherwise it loses the character of

the Mazourka, to which family of steps it
belongs.

Cellarius thus analyzes the Redowa in
turning:

"*Jeté* on the left foot in passing before the
lady as in the *Valse a trois temps*, gliding with
the right foot behind to the fourth position
on side, the left foot is then brought back to
the third position behind; the *pas de Basque*
is performed with the right foot in carrying
the right foot forward, and you recommence
with the left foot."

The *pas de Basque* ought to be done in three
equal times, as in the Mazourka. This is the
way that it is taught in Paris and London.
Many of our Waltzers begin with sliding the
left foot first, [one;] bring the right foot up
behind, [2;] and then throw the left back of
right, and bring the right foot up before,
[3;] ready to repeat the same to right.

THE GORLITZA.

The Gorlitza is danced by two like the Waltz. The music is two-four-time. This dance may be divided into four different steps.

1. One bar of the Polka in turning half round, and the same without turning, finishing on both feet; the left foot forward for the lady as well as for the Gentleman.

2. *Sissonne* with the left foot for both lady and gentleman, and two little *pas marche* behind, in turning. This to be repeated.

3. One complete step of the Polka Mazourka.

4. *Tems levé* sideways, *Sissonne*, and *pas de bourré* behind and before. [This is the Polka Mazourka.]

N. B. For those not acquainted with the foreign terms for dancing, a few lessons will be required to make them understood.

STEP OF THE VALSE A DEUX TEMPS.

The music of this Valse contains three times, like the plain or old waltz, only they are otherwise divided and accented, two of the times being included in one; or rather, one of the times being divided into two. The first step consists of a *glissade*, the second is a *chassée*, including two times in one.

The Gentleman begins by sliding to the left with his left foot, then performing a *chassee* towards the left with the right foot, without turning at all during the first two times. He then slides backwards with his right leg, turning half round; after which he puts his left leg behind to perform with it a *chassée* forward, again turning half round at the same time. He must finish with his right foot forward, and begin again with his left foot as before.

To dance the *Deux Temps* well it must be danced with short steps, the feet sliding so smoothly over the surface of the floor that they scarcely ever seem to be raised above it. Anything like springing or jumping is altogether inadmissible; moreover, though a very

Valse à Deux Temps.

quick dance, it must be danced very quietly
and elegantly, and every inclination to romping or other vulgar movements must be carefully checked and corrected. This is the be-
setting sin of dancing ; a sin, however, which
is committed by bad dancers only, because it
is easier to do anything wrong than to do it
right or well.

A gentleman should practise this dance
long in private before he attempts it in public,
if not quite *au fait ;* and he subjects his partners to all sorts of inconveniences, not to
speak of kicks and bruises. Many bold,
foolish, or conceited young men, misled by
the apparent easiness of the step, undertake
to lead a lady through the Valses after a few
lessons ; and, perhaps to their own great
satisfaction, they do get through them. But
little are they aware of the discomfort, perhaps pain, which they occasion ; and if they
only saw themselves in a glass—what hob-
nails and clodpoles they look—they would
blush at the inferior position which they occupy in a gay and accomplished assembly.

The *Deux Temps* should not be danced
long without stopping ; for after a few turns
it becomes laborious, and where labor is very
apparent, grace is wanting.

Tall gentlemen should avoid, if possible,
waltzing with short ladies, as their difference
in height, must necessarily destroy the ease

of blended movement, which should act like
one person.

The vivacity of the new Valses, has infused
increased animation and speed into the old
Valse à *Trois Temps*, or, " plain waltz," as
it is called with us.   They even attempt to
reverse it—a very awkward movement.

THE VALSE A CINQ TEMPS.

Five Step Waltz.

AS DESCRIBED BY CELLARIUS.

The gentleman's step.

First time.—He should have his right foot in front, make a *Jeté* with the left foot passing before the lady, as in the Valse *à Trois Temps.*

Second time.—Place the right foot in the third position behind.

Third time.—Join the left foot behind the right.

Fourth time—Bring the right foot forward in the fourth position.

Fifth time.—A little glissade behind and on the side.

The waltzer must always recommence with the left foot. In the three times the waltzer must make a half turn, as in the old three time waltz; scarcely turn at all in the fourth, and make the second half turn in the fifth, upon the little glissade.

The lady thus—First time.—She should have her left foot in front, make a *Jeté* upon the right foot, lifting the left foot behind.

Second time.—*Coupé* upon the left foot, lifting the right foot before to the fourth position.

Third time.—*Jeté* upon the right foot lifting the left behind.

Fourth time.—*Jeté* with the left foot, lifting the right behind.

Fifth time.—Little glissade behind with the right foot.

The lady should not forget that she must always begin with the right foot.

This Valse is susceptible of as many variations as the others, and admits of the *l'envers* and *l'endroit*, viz :—left and right.

MAZOURKA VALSE.

THE CELLERIUS VALSE.

This is a slow and extremely graceful dance, though it may suffer in comparison with its gay and sprightly *compagnons*, la Valses, Polka and Schottische, yet it has many admirers.

It consists of three parts, which we describe thus :

1. Spring with the right foot, at the same advancing left foot, [count two ;] then spring on the left foot, [count one ;] spring again on the left foot, at the same time advancing right foot, [count two ;] spring again on the right foot, [count one.] These six steps complete one circle.

2d. Take your position; spring on the right foot, at the same time striking with the heels together; slide left foot to the left, bending the knee, [count two ;] then bring right foot up to the place of the left foot, with a slight hop, raising the left, [count one ;] then spring again on the right foot, striking the two heels, sliding the left foot to the left, [count two,] falling on the left foot, and raising the right behind, [count one ;]

then spring on the left foot and reverse the whole of the second part.

3d. Spring on right foot, at the same slideing left foot to the left, [counting two;] then hop on the left foot, bringing right foot up behind left foot, [count one;] then spring on the left foot and slide right foot to the right, [count two;] then bring the left foot to the place of the right foot with a hop, raising right foot, [count one.]

These details constitute the steps for the gentleman. For the lady the steps are precisely similar—but reversed—thus, for right foot read left; and for left, right.

GALLOPADE—LE GALOP.

Is a dance now very much in vogue, from
its being so very similar to the Valse *à Deux
Temps* in appearance; but the music is extremely different, being in two-four time.
Like the round dances, an unlimited number
may join, and the step is somewhat similar
to the *Chassez*. The gentleman commences
with his left foot, and the lady with her right,
and it is generally commenced with eight
sliding steps, the gentleman keeping his left
foot forward, and the lady her right; then
half turn, and *Vice Versâ*, the gentleman
with right foot forward, and the lady with
left, and so at pleasure. It may be varied by
valsing. This dance is generally used as a
finale, or, concludes the first part of a public
ball. It is of a very exciting nature.

WALTZ QUADRILLE.

1. Leading and opposite couples right and left.

The same couples set and swing partners half round with right hands.

Again set and swing back to places, giving left hands.

All *poussette* round to places.   *Viz. Waltz.*

2d. Leading couple promenade within the figure, and turn partners into places.

Ladies chain—all promenade quite round.

3d. Leading and opposite couples cross over, giving right hands.

The side couples do the same.

All set and turn partners half round.

All promenade to places—all poussette quite round to places

THE WALTZ COTILLION.

A pleasing little dance—places as in a Quadrille. Leading and side couples. It may be learned in a few minutes, to those who waltz, there being only one figure, repeated by each couple. The figure is as follows :—

The first couple valse inside the figure with either the "plain waltz" step, or *Deux Temps*, at pleasure, finishing at their places, and occupying eight bars.

The first and opposite ladies cross over with a valse step, [eight bars ;] the first and second gentlemen do likewise ; the third and fourth ladies repeat this figure, and then their partners ; the top and bottom couples then valse to places, [four bars ;] side couples do likewise.

Each gentleman then takes his partner's right hand, and they both advance to each other with a valse step, [one bar,] and then retire, [one bar ;] the gentleman then passes the lady under his right, and she passes to the next gentleman, and he passes to the next lady in the same manner as the grand chain, in the Lancers , or, right and left all

eight—[this occupies two bars with each.]
This figure is repeated with every lady, until
all regain their respective places, [taking
thirty-two bars;] side couples separate, and
join hands with top and bottom couples,
forming four in a line; all advance and retire
twice, [four bars;] then all cross over and
turn, [taking four bars;] then re-advance and
re-retire twice, (four bars,) and re-cross over
to places, (four bars.) The four couples then
valse round to places.

This completes the figure, but it is repeated four times, each couple in succession
taking the lead.

This, though a most graceful and easy
dance, has been put aside by the more
fashionable round dances. In England it is
very often introduced in private circles. The
figures are easily followed; one or two couples
knowing them is sufficient to keep it up.

We have occasionally introduced this dance
in our *Soirées*, and varied its character by
using the Polka step instead of the plain
valse.

This variety has generally given satisfaction, as it makes an agreeable change from
the Quadrille and round dances. If danced
to the valse step, the music should be moder-
ately fast only, as if too quick, it destroys the
gracefulness of the dance.

CIRCULAR WALTZ.

The party form a circle, then promenade during the introduction; all waltz sixteen bars, set, holding partner's right hand and turn, waltz thirty-two bars, rest and turn partners slowly, face partner and *chassez* to right and left, *pirouette* [turn] lady twice with right hand, all waltz sixteen bars, set and turn, all form a circle, still retaining the lady by the right hand, and move round to the left, sixteen bars, waltz to *finale*.

CIRCASSIAN CIRCLE.

The company are arranged in couples round the room, the ladies being placed on the right of the gentlemen, after which the first and second lead off the dance, facing each other; at the conclusion, the first couples with the fourth, and the second with the third couple recommence the figure, and so on until they go completely round the circle, when the dance is concluded.

HIGHLAND REEL.

This merry dance can be performed by two couples; but, being a favorite, the admission of many is not unusual. The company form parties of three along the room, the lady's position being between two gentlemen, and fronting the opposite three; all then advance and retire, each lady executing the reel with her right hand partner, and then with her left hand partner to places; hands three round, and back again; all six advance and retire; after which lead through to the next three, continuing the figure to the end of the room.

The figure may be formed with four in a line.

Adopt the Highland step and music.

SPANISH DANCE.

This very easy and beautiful waltzing dance, once a favorite of our ball rooms, is now seldom called for; it has been supplanted by the Polka and other round dances: it is occasionally introduced at private parties; but it may be revived, and, therefore, we give it here.

The couples stand as for a country dance, [sometimes the couples are arranged in a circle,] except that the first gentleman must be on the ladies' side, and the first lady on the gentlemen's side; and to prevent the other couples waiting, every fourth lady and gentleman exchange places. By this means delay is prevented, and the whole can start at once in the next movement.

The first gentleman and second lady advance and retire with a valse step, and change places. First lady and second gentleman do likewise at the same time.

First gentleman and partner advance and retire with valse step, and exchange places. Second gentleman and partner do likewise at the same time.

First gentleman and partner repeat the

same.   First lady and second gentleman do the same at the same time.

All four join hands, and advance to centre, and return: pass ladies to the left.   All join hands again, and advance to the centre as before, and pass ladies to the left.   This is repeated twice more.   Each gentleman takes his own partner, and the two couples valse round each other once or twice, *ad libitum*, leaving the second lady and gentleman at the top of the dance, as in a country dance.

The first lady and gentleman repeat the same figure with every succeeding couple to the end of dance.

But the whole line may be put in motion at once; it is better and more lively.   The standing still so long is the objection to the English country dances.

COULON'S QUADRILLE.

OR

DOUBLE QUADRILLE.

Introduced by that teacher in London, in 1851.

This Quadrille is to be danced by four couples only. All Cotillion music will suit it, excepting that the half only is required. It is exceedingly easy to learn, having the same figures as the common Quadrille, but it is arranged to be danced by four instead of two, which makes the Quadrille last only half the time of the other, and four figures, which look more complicated and pretty than the old set.

Figure 1—*Le Pantalon.*

The top and bottom couples *chaine Anglaise*, or right and left, towards the centre, whilst the two side couples dance *Grande Chaine* round them.

All set and turn their partners.

The four ladies, ladies chain or hands across which makes a kind of *Moulinet*.

All half promenade, the top and bottom couples *Chaine Anglaise* in the centre, while the side couples *Grande Chaine* round them.

Figure II.—*L' Ete*.

The gentleman at the top, and the one on his right, begin with their opposite ladies and dance the figure of *l' été*. (See page 31.)

Figure III.—*La Poule*.

This is nearly "Right hand across," with us. (See page 31.)

Figure IV.—*La Pastorale*.

(See page 32.)

The top gentleman with his partner, and the gentleman opposite, with his partner, dance the figure of *La Pastorale* with the two couples on their right in the corner of the room.

☞ That is with their respective side couples—"a new mode of dancing that figure," which is the "Cauliflower."

GRACE FIGURE.

In Cauliflower Cotillion

103

Figure V.—Finale.

All Gallopade round.

The top and bottom couples gallopade forward, and while returning backwards, the side couples do the same forward, and when these go back the others advance, then the top and bottom couples cross over, and after them the side couples do the same. (This figure is to be repeated from the beginning.] Ladies chain by the four ladies. All Gallopade round. Repeat the same figure. The side couple begin the second time. All Gallopade to conclude.

POLKA QUADRILLES.

No. 1.—Leading couples promenade forward, (4 bars,) changing heads, promenade back—(4 bars.) The same couples double waltz around each other (8 bars,) *Balancé en carré*—or waltz in places (8 bars.) The same couples double waltz again—(8 bars.) Side couples do the same.

No. 2.—The top couple waltz up to the opposite couple—(8 bars.) The same couples pass into each others places by four polka steps going one away—4 steps sit back—the ladies passing in the centre, the gents outside (8 bars.) The top couple waltz to their places. (8 bars.) The other couples do the same.

No. 3.—The top couple waltz around the side couple on their right, finishing in front of them, (8 bars:) The same hands across half round with right hands, (4 bars,) back again with left hands, (4 bars.) Top couple then waltz back to their places (8 bars.) The top and bottom couples then double waltz around each other to places, [8 bars.]

The other couples do the same.

Note.—The side couple on the right of the top couple begin the figure now, so round.

No. 4.—The top couple forward with Polka Waltz, passing before their *Vis-à-Vis* (8 bars.) The two couples then form hands four and execute the passes—thus all point their toes, the gents their left ones, the ladies their right ones, and breaking hands pass into each others places. They all then point their reverse toes and pass again into their first places. This is done four times, taking (8 bars.)

The top couple waltz to places (8 bars.) The bottom and side couples do the same.

No. 5.—The grand round—four couples promenade or waltz round, (8 bars.)

All *Balanceé en carré*, or waltz in places, at pleasure (8 bars.)

The leading couple then waltz back to centre of Quadrille, and back again to places, (8 bars ;) the same waltz around inside of figure (8 bars.) All grand round again (8 bars.)

The same figures repeated by the other couples, successively around.

☞ These Quadrilles are only danced so in Philadelphia. The heel and toe is now omitted with us, and the toe only pointed—it is more simple and in better taste. The arms akimbo is no longer practised. Every figure is now waltzed.

LANCERS.

EIGHT BARS REST TO EACH QUADRILLE.

No. 1 *La Rose.*

Lady and Gent *chassé* to right and left,
the same swing all round once to places ; (8
bars) [tiroir] top couple with hands joined
gallop into the bottom couples place, while
the bottom couple pass outside of the former
couple into their place—both couples gallop
back to their own places, the bottom couple
passing through the centre, the top couple
passing outside to places (8 bars.) Four gentlemen hands across with left hands, keeping
their ladies by their right hands, with their
right hands, the whole thus forming a cross,
and set—then turn the ladies to centre, who
also form left hands across, as the gentlemen
did (8 bars.) The ladies then group their
right hands together, elevated, while the left
hands are lowered and joined together—forming the cage figure—move once round, and
turn their partners [8 bars.]

The other couples do the same—making four times.

The whole will take 128 bars, four times repeated.

No. 2 *La Lodoiska.*

Top lady and bottom gentleman *chassé* forward and retire ; partners *chassée* across and back ; turn partners : *Balancé* to corner partners—form a line of four at sides, the line advances and retires, turn partners to places. The other couples do the same.

No. 3 *La Dorset.*

Top lady forward and stop, then the gent, opposite forward and halt ; top lady then returns to place, then the gent returns to place. The same *chassé-de-chassé*—the ladies double chain—viz : The four ladies hands across once round, and then cross their left hands to return back again. Their partners then take their ladies' right hands with their own right hands and place their left hands on the waist of their ladies, thus forming a cross, all return round to places, ending by turning partners. The other couples do the same—always ending with the figure of the cross.

No. 4. *Nina.*

The top lady and gentleman, with her corner partner, (the gent on her right,) form the grace figure, while the bottom couple do the same, taking the gent on her right hand, and thus the six persons will advance twice up to each other—on returning the second time the lady will courtesy to the gentlemen on each side of her. Then hands three once round, and turn partners. The side ladies perform the same figures. Then the gentlemen respectively, taking always their own partner and the lady on their left hand.

No. 5. *Finale.*—*Les Lanciers*

The Grand chain, viz. :—Right and left all eight; [this occupies sixteen bars.] The leading couple promenade inside the figure, and return to their own places, finishing with their faces turned outside the Quadrille. The side couples fall in behind. They, and bottom couples remain as they were, the whole forming two lines ; the gentlemen on one side and the ladies on the other, [eight bars.] They all *chassez croisez*, (the ladies to the left, the gentlemen to the right,) the gentlemen passing behind their own partners. Ladies then to the right, and gentlemen to left, [occupying eight bars.] "The leading lady leads off to the right—the leading gent off to the left, being followed in single file by those dancers behind them. They meet at the bottom of the Quadrille and pass up to their own places, [8 bars.] The four ladies join hands, and the four gentlemen do likewise, facing partners ; all advance and retire, and each turns partner to place, [eight bars.] Grand chain to begin each time. The other couples then repeat this.

The set now ends with the grand chain, or a promenade.

Note.

The grand square, which used to end these Quadrilles, is now omitted in London, being found too difficult of execution in the ballroom. This is to be regretted, as it was a very beautiful movement. It is now danced as above.

The Lancers are not often danced, for the reason that the figures are somewhat intricate and difficult, and require to be taught—a single individual not knowing the movement throws out the rest—they can only be properly acquired through the medium of a capable instructor ; they cannot be picked up, like the " plain Cotillions," and awkwardly paced through in the most ungraceful manner, as is the unblushing custom in our ballrooms, and with untaught dancers.

There are several sets of these quadrilles. Those that we here give, have been introduced into some of our dancing schools and parties, and, we think, they are the best.

THE ORIGINAL SCHOTTISCHE QUADRILLES.

FIGURES.

1st. Quad.—Eight bars rest between each Quadrille.

Top couple Schottische valse up to their *Vis à Vis*, [eight bars.] The leading couples thus together, give their right hands and set and turn half round, [four bars,] then set and give left hands and turn back, [four bars,] making eight bars for that figure.

Top couple then Schottische valse back to places, [eight bars;] the leading couples half promenade, and four *jeté voltes* to places, [eight bars.] The two couple in places execute the *pas marché* [beating] waltz, [eight bars.]

The other couples do the same.

2d. Quadrille.

The two leading couples—the gents taking the ladies by their left hand, and *balauce* and pass into each others places with gallop step, [the ladies passing in centre,] [eight

bars.] The same *chassez* across to corners,
[four bars;] *balancé* with corner partners
giving right hands and turn half round, (four
bars.) Again give left hands and turn to
places, (four bars.) The leading couples *re-chassez* to places left.

Then the same *balancé*, and return to places,
as in the first figure; the ladies passing in
centre, (eight bars.)

The same couples end with the beating
waltz, (eight bars.)

The side couples perform the same.

3d. Quadrille.

The ladies in these figures are changed all
round. Top couple Schottische valse up to
their right hand side couple, (eight bars;)
set and exchange partners; the top gentleman takes the side lady and galops out to
the centre of the Cotillion, and then waltzes
to the bottom couple, (eight bars;) exchange
ladies again; the top gentleman will take the
leading lady in the bottom couple and waltz
with her to the side couple on his left, (doing
the rocking valse,) (eight bars;) exchange
ladies thus.—top gentleman takes the left
side lady, and with beating valse waltz to his
own place, (eight bars.) The ladies thus all
changed, all in places do the rocking valse,
(eight bars.)

All the gentlemen, successively round, do the same figures, till the fourth gentleman regains his partner.

4th. Quadrille.

The two leading couples forward together with Schottische valse, (eight bars.) The two gents take each others partners and valse back to their places, (four bars;) a pause of two bars; promenade up to each other, (four bars;) retake partners, and valse back to places, (four bars.) The same couples do the rocking valse, (eight bars.)

The side couples do the same.

The second part of the figure.

The two leading ladies go off right, and cross into each others places, using four *volte* steps, (four bars,) followed by their gentlemen; when across, the gents chase their ladies around in places, (four bars;) then the gents take their partners in valse position, and execute the beating valse, (eight bars;) the ladies again go off right, chased by their partners to places, and the little chase round in places as before, (eight bars;) the same couples end with rocking valse, (eight bars.)

Side couples do the same.

5th. *Quadrille.*

Grand rond. The four couples begin by the *Schottische balancé* in places, (four bars,) and all gallopade half round Quadrille, (four bars;) resume *balancé* and gallop to places, (eight bars;) this rond takes (sixteen bars;) all together *pas marche valse*, viz: beating waltz; the leading couple within the figure perform the Schottische valse, (sixteen bars,) ending in places; all together do the rocking valse, (eight bars.) The solo figure is done by every couple regularly around, preceded and followed by all the general figures as described. Each figure is of course executed four times.

They occupy about fifteen minutes in dancing.

The Schottische valse is preserved throughout the set.

JUNIOR SCHOTTISCHE QUADRILLE.

*Danced to one air; or, changes may be made
in the music at pleasure.*

1st. Figure.

Top and bottom couples promenade around
each other inside of figure.   (Eight bars.)
The same couples waltz across into each
others places.   (Eight bars.)
The side couples do the same figures.
(Eight bars.)
All waltz round to places.   (Eight bars.)

2d. Figure.—Eight bars rest.

Top and bottom couples promenade up, and
exchange ladies.   Gents with the ladies thus
exchanged waltz back to places, (eight bars.)
All the couples *allemand*, thus: the gentlemen swing the ladies half round with right
hands, (four bars,) and back with left hands,
(four bars,) in places (eight bars.)   The side
couples do the same.   Exchange ladies, (eight
bars.   All thus again *allemand* in places.
The leading couples meet again, and the

gentlemen regain their own partners, **and** valse into each others places. [Eight bars.]

The side couples do the same. [Eight bars]

All being in opposite places, waltz round to their own places. [Eight bars.]

3d. Figure.—*Eight bars rest.*

The leading couples promenade up to their respective left hand side couples, [four bars.]

The four gents take the ladies thus brought opposite to them, and waltz out to their left hand sides, forming a line of four across the room—the leading couples in the centre of line—the side couples outside. This takes, [four bars.]

The two lines forward, each meeting thus their partners, take partners and waltz to places. [Eight bars.]

The side couples repeat the same, taking care to form the line up and down the room. The side couples are now in the centre of line. [Eight bars.]

4th Figure.

1.—*Double Lady's Chain*—The four ladies hands across half round [4 bars,] on reaching

the gentlemen opposite their places they waltz
in place (or, swing with left hand,) with him
(4 bars.)

The four gents then also right hands across,
'till they reach their respective ladies, (4 bars)
then waltz with partners in places, (4 bars,)
all waltz round to their own places. (8 bars.)

5th Figure. Eight bars rest.

Grand Chain—viz : Right and left all eight.
The gentlemen waltzing with every third lady
he meets (4 bars,) in going round—which will
be four times—(32 bars.)

The top and bottom couples *balancé* to their
respective right hand side couples and do the
tiroir figure—the two couples pass through
each other in open order, the ladies passing
in centre, with four turning Voltes—the gentlemen pass outside—thus they pass around
the Quadrille, doing the *Schottische Balancé*
and four Voltes with each couple they meet,
till they arrive in places, taking four times
for the passes—(32 bars.)

Finish with the Schottische Valse,[16 bars.]
Waltzing *ad libitum.*

MAZOURKA QUADRILLES.

These beautiful Quadrilles are not as much danced as they should be, the reason may be found, in the difficulty of their easy acquirement. The steps are simple as well as the figures, but of course, require careful practice with proper instruction ; two potent objections to our ball-room dancers, who have a repugnance to attempt anything of a novel character, that involves trouble and time in learning.

In Europe, these Mazourkas are so constructed that, they may be danced by two couples, or by as many as the room will contain—that is, the two couples stand opposite to each other, as in a Cotillion, only omitting the side couples, and standing up and down the room forming two lines. When danced with an easy grace, they are a very pleasing and decorous dance, not admitting of the vulgarities of the Polkas.

There are many figures to these dances, principally based on the old Cotillion—but few of them have been introduced with us.

The *Mazourka Quadrilles* introduced by Mons. Hazzard, teacher of dancing, formerly of this city, and as it is danced at most of the public balls here, it is thought proper to give the figures. It is a long dance, taking from eighteen to twenty minutes.

KNEELING ATTITUDE.

In Mazourka Quadrille.

PHILADELPHIA MAZOURKA QUADRILLES.

1 *Quadrille—8 bars rest between each one.*

1. *Kolo*—Viz. : All hands round to left, [4 bars,] back to places [4 bars.]

2. *Tour-sur-place*—All four couples [4 bars.]

3. *Holubiec*—That is a waltz in places, [4 bars.]
This is also done in places by all.

4. The top couple promenade around inside of Quadrille—gent having his lady in his right hand, [8 bars.]

5. The same couple, execute the square, [4 bars.]

6. The same end with Holubiec Waltz, [4 bars.]
Each of the other couples do the same.

2d Quadrille.

1. *For Kolo*—All do the Mazourka Valse round, [16 bars.]
There are four changes in this round.

2. The top couples go off to right hand side couples, and 4 hands once round, [8 bars.]

3. The same couple then go to the bottom leading couple, [with the Mazourka step 4 bars,] and hands across, once round, [4 bars,] 8 bars in all.

4. The same couple go to their left hand side couple, making [4 bars,] and with that couple right and left, [4 bars.]

5. The same couples promenade to places, [4 bars.]

6. When in places *Holubiec*, that is, the waltz as before, [4 bars.]

The other couples do the same. The whole 48 bars.

3d Quadrille.

1. *Kolo*—Thus the four couples Mazourka Valse all round, making eight turns, [8 bars.]

2. *The Grace Figure*—The top gentleman leads his lady out with her left hand in his right hand, and passes her round in his front to his left side, holding her *left* hand in his *left* hand, and then extends his right hand to the side lady on his right. Takes thus the side lady's right hand, while the two ladies will join their disengaged hands together, behind his back—this takes [4 bars.]

Thus grouped, in what is termed the *Grace Figure*—they execute a promenade of [4 bars.]

He then turns the two ladies under his arms, and all grouping together their hands, holding them up and facing each other, the three perform a round to left [4 bars,] and back again to right, [4 bars.] The gentleman will then leave the lady in his left hand, in the place of the side lady he took from thence —this figure each time, takes [16 bars.]

The same gentleman in the same way takes the bottom leading lady, and performs the same figure with her and the right side lady he took at first, and leaves the latter lady in the bottom lady's place. He then takes the fourth lady and bottom leading lady and does the same figures, leaving the latter lady in the fourth lady's place, and then leads the fourth lady to his own place, and *Holubiecs* with her [4 bars.]

All the gentlemen respectively around the Quadrille execute the same figures 'till the four ladies are returned to places.

4th. Quadrille.

1. *Kolo.*—Thus all the couples promenade,
viz. :—Partners in hand, when half round,
all *tour-sur-place*, (4 bars.) Continue promenade to places, and then *tour-sur-place*,
(4 bars.) This takes (16 bars.)

2. *Tiroir Figure.*—Thus the two leading
couples make a half turn in places, and glide
sideways into each others places : The ladies
passing in centre, the two gentlemen outside
The gents again take their ladies in waltz position, make a half turn as before ; and in the
same way re-pass into places, (8 bars.)

3. The leading couples then swing round in
places with right hands and then with left
hands. (8 bars.)

The side couples do the same.

This figure is repeated by the leading couples, and also by the sides.

5th Quadrille.

1. *Kolo.*—*Grand Rond*, as in the first one,
(8 bars.)

2. All together, *tour-sur-place*, (4 bars.)

3. *Holubiec.*—(8 bars.)

4. All right and left round—gentlemen walt-zing, with every third lady they meet in going round.

This right and left is not done by giving hands. The gentlemen fold their arms—they pass two ladies in going round, and the third lady they meet, will *Holubiec* [or waltz] with her [4 bars.] This done four times in each quarter of the Cotillion. The last time in his own place with partner.

The *Grand Chain* thus takes [32 bars.]

Finis.

RUSSIAN MAZOURKA QUADRILLES.

DESCRIPTION OF THE FIVE FIGURES.

Introduction.—Wait eight bars.

1. *Kolo*, or, the Grand round—all taking hands—four steps to L, four steps to R, or back to places. [Eight bars.]

The step thus used is the *Waltz Mazourka*, with the *Coup de talon*, which can be done in moving sideways, or in waltzing.

2. Grand chain, half round and return to places with the Mazourka step. [Eight bars.]

3. Figure part begins. Top couple goes out with Mazourka step and two *Pas de Basque* steps, [four bars,] and Redowa Valse to places. [Four bars.]

4. The same couple [*Holubiec*,] thus :—Pas de Basque around each other in places, and Mazourka valse. [Eight bars.]

The other couples do the same figures.

2d. *Figure.*

1. *Kolo.* The four couples in waltz position, go round with the Mazourka sliding heel

and stroke step, [*viz: Coup de talon*,] done three times, and for the fourth time one whole waltz turn; this is executed four times in going round, and four waltz turns in each *quatre* of the Quadrille; or at the end of every four bars a waltz turn, [sixteen bars.]

2. The leading couples in waltz position, glide around each other with sliding Mazourka step, to their respective right hand side couples, [4 bars.] and with the sides perform the *Tiroir Figure*—this is simply a *Chassez Croisez*, the gents and ladies facing their own partners, [ladies passing in centre] 2 bars, one way and [2 bars] back again.

4. The leading couples then hands four in centre, [4 bars.]

5. Redowa Valse to places, [4 bars.]

6. Holubiec in places—the Redowa step done as a square, and the partners disengaged —finish with Valse, [8 bars.]

☞ The side couples execute the same figures.

SECOND PART OF SAME QUADRILLE.

1. The leading couples do the Cellarius Valse movement, [so called,] [16 bars.]

☞ This figure cannot be easily described, and must be taught.

2. The same couples Holubiec in places, [8 bars.]   Viz. :—*Jeté Volte, Pas de Bourré back.*

Sides repeat the same.

3d. Figure.

1. *Kolo.*—The four couples together perform the *Tiroir figure* all round to places, [8 bars.]

2. The leading couple Valse out [4 bars,] gentleman takes the right hand side lady, and with his own partner executes the "Graces," which takes [24 bars.]

This is only done *once* by each gentleman, going regularly round.

This figure must be taught.

4th. Figure.

1. *Kolo.*—All the couples promenade round with the forward Mazourka step, and *Pas de Basque,* half round the Quadrille, [8 bars,] and Redowa Valse to places, [8 bars.]

2. The leading couples *Tiroir,* into each others places, [4 bars.]

3. Set to partners with Mazourka step, [4 bars.]

4. Re-traversez to places, with the same figure, [4 bars.]

5. Set again to partners in places with **Ma**-zourka step.

Side couples do the same.

SECOND PART OF FIGURE.

1. The two leading couples cross over with Mazourka and *Pas de Basque* steps, [8 bars.]
2. Redowa Valse to places, [8 bars.]

☞ Sides the same.

5th. Figure.

1. *The Kolo* is as the first Quadrille—all eight hands round.
2. All the gentlemen *Allemand* with their partners in places, ending with casting their ladies to their left hand corners, while they go to the right hand corners, each meeting at the corners a lady and gentleman.   This takes [8 bars.]
3. The ladies and gentlemen thus meeting, [partners being changed all round,] *Pas de Basque* around each other, [4 bars.]   The lady being thus left on the right of the gentleman, they will join hands and with the forward Mazourka step promenade half round Quadrille, [4 bars,] and casts the lady thus with

him to left hand corner, where new partners are met as before—where all execute the *Pas de Basque* again, and promenade half round. These changes of partners are done four times, with the same steps and figures, till the gentleman regain their own partners.

Salute partners and FINI.

Note.

The steps of this dance are nearly the same as those of the old Mazourka set, only the *Pas de Basque* and Redowa Valse steps are combined with them, making it a light and elegant Mazourka set, being less fatiguing and much shorter than the other Quadrilles. They are easily acquired, but must be taught, no written or choregraphical description can convey them accurately to the pupil. Like all dances and steps they must be learned, Books can only assist the Amateur and learner.

Explanation of the signs :— ● Gentleman. ○ Lady. Give hands . . . . . . Figures— - - - ●

GERMAN OR PARLOR COTILLION.

Those Cotillions may be danced with the step, either of the Waltz, the Polka, the Mazourka or the *Vàlse à Deux Temps*, by an unlimited number of persons.

Each gentleman places his partner on his right hand. There is no rule that any particular figure shall be danced, nor is it intended that the figures here explained shall be danced in rotation. The selection is left to the determination of the leading couple, who commence the figure, which the other couples repeat in succession. In large parties of twenty-four or thirty couples, it is customary for two or more couples to perform one figure at the same time, otherwise the amusement might be tedious by its length.

To preserve the regularity of the dance, the same seat should be maintained by each individual throughout.

It must be well understood that in selecting partners for the figures hereafter explained, no previous introduction between the parties is requisite. It is only necessary to present the hand to the lady or gentleman who is chosen.

One great interest in these figures is, that their constant variety enables each gentleman to dance with almost every lady.

The first couple start with the Polka, or Valse, and are immediately followed by all the other couples.

After one round the places are resumed, and what may be called the first figure is begun.

First Figure.

The leader selects two ladies, and his partner selects two gentlemen. Thus :

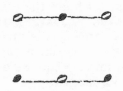

They advance, and each gentleman takes the lady opposite to him, and dances one or two rounds with her, after which they return to their places. The next couple do after the same manner, and if, as I said before, the Cotillion be a large one, two or more couples begin at the same time.

The Pyramid.

The first three couples begin with the Polka or Waltz round the room.   The first three ladies choose three other ladies, and the six ladies place themselves thus :

The three gentlemen then select three other gentlemen and holding each others hands pass in zig zag form between the ladies ; when on a signal given by the leader, each gentleman takes one of the ladies standing, and dances the Polka with her.   When they have resumed their seats, the other three couple repeat the same figure, and so on till all the couples have danced it.

The Two Flowers.

The leader takes two ladies, and asks them each to name a flower. He then presents them to one of the gentlemen, desiring him to say which flower he prefers. When the gentleman has made his choice, he is presented with the lady the name of whose flower he guessed—he dances with her, and the leader dances with the other lady round the room. The other couples perform the same figure in their turn.

The Round and Grand Chain.

The first two couples dance several rounds of the Mazourka, and Petit Tour. The first gentleman then takes another lady, and the second lady takes another gentleman, thus:

They then advance and retire, advance again, and the two gentlemen with the lady pass under the arms of the two ladies facing them thus :

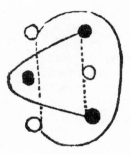

And join hands behind the gentleman. The ladies also join hands behind the centre lady thus :

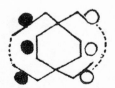

They turn one round to the left, afterwards
form a circle holding hands. Then *Grand
Chaine* until they meet their partners, when
they couple off with the Mazourka.   The same
figure for the remaining couples.

The Star.

The first three couples commence with the
Polka.   The ladies select three other gentlemen, and the gentlemen three other ladies.
The six ladies place themselves in a *moulinet*
right hands in the centre, giving the left
hands to the gentlemen, and all turn thus :

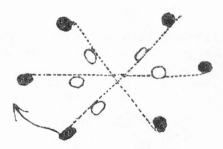

Three of the ladies hold their hands a little
above those of the other three.

At a given signal the three ladies who hold

their hands above, leave the centre and dance with their partners in the narrow space between each lady and gentleman.

Meanwhile the three other couples continue to turn slowly one way and the other, still keeping in the centre of the star, changing from right hands to left thus:

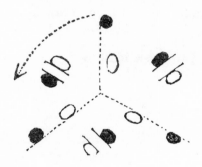

After repeating this two or three times, they finish with a round of the Polka, and return to their places. The same to be repeated by the rest.

SUPPLEMENTAL NEW DANCES.

Embracing the most recently fashionable
Valses and Quadrilles of Parisan origin, and,
as danced in the London and Paris drawing-
rooms.   They are light, neat and elegant, and
acquired in a few lessons.

ESPAGNOLE.

A VALSE CACHUCHA

*Composed by R. Renausy, of the Imperial
Academy of Music Paris.*

DESCRIPTION OF STEP.

Coupé with left foot by gent.   *Sauté* on
right foot, *jeté on left foot*, *Sauté* on same foot,
right foot in the rear, *ensemblé*, *Glissé* left foot,

follow with right foot and *Coupé* with right foot. *Sauté* left foot, right foot in the air. *Pas de Basque* with right foot, *Coupé* with right foot, *Sauté* on left foot. Repeat the *Pas de Basque* and *Coupé*, ending with a *Sauté* to re-commence again.

For the lady the directions are the same only reversing the feet.

L' ANGLICANE.

A VALSE.

By R. Renausy, of the Imperial Academy of Music.

The Step.—This dance is executed to two-fourth time, [*moderato.*] It is danced in waltz position, turning in the usual mode, or reversing at pleasure.

1st. The gent slides his left foot to the left, [counting one,] *Coupé* under with the right foot.

2d. *Balonné* with left foot.

3d. *Jeté* with left foot.

4th. To turn with the lady, the gentleman *assemblé* with right foot behind; sissonne with right foot and *assemblé* again behind.

The lady uses the reverse feet, making the *l'Assemblé* before, viz. : throwing her left foot before the right. The dancers may reverse the turn at pleasure, like other Valses.

VARSOVIANA VALSE.

143

VARSOVIANA.

A VALSE MAZOURKA

Danced in Waltz Position.

This Valse is composed of two movements and two steps.   The music makes the change.

1st. Part.—As thus—a *Chassé*, a half turn finishing with an *appel;* and an interval of one note, counts six.   The *Theorem* of the step may be thus laid down.

The gent *Glissé* with left foot [count one,] follow with right foot, [count 2,] *Glissé* with left foot [3,] then make a half turn on left toe [changing sides with lady,] [counting 4,] *Appel* with right foot, [viz.: point toe of right foot,] [count 5,] rest thus the interval of one note, [count 6.]   This step is done four times.

2d. Part.—The gent and lady now move off with the *Coup de talon* Mazourka step.   Thus the gent *Glissé* with left foot [count 1,] follow with right foot [count 2,] strike left heel on

right heel sharply count (3.) This takes
eight bars, finish with one or two *Pas Marché*
steps. *Holubiec* once round (8 bars.) using
the same step.

Repeat the same till change of music—so
the two parts are executed alternately.

Note.—The lady takes the reverse feet.—
The Valse position is never disengaged.

Note.

The dancers have adopted a *Pas Marché*
style in executing this Valse.

VARSOVIANA VALSE.

HUNGROISE.

A VALSE MAZOURKA.

The gentleman and lady go off with the Mazourka heel step. To begin, gent strikes his left heel on right heel [1,] then slides the left foot forward, [2,] follow with right foot [3.] The lady using the reverse foot.

For the second step, the gentleman makes a *Pas de Basque* backward and the lady forward, they then make two *jetés*—the gent falls on his right foot and the lady on her left foot, and then *jeté* on their other feet, leaving the gent's right foot up and the lady's left foot up, to go off again with the first step of the dance.

The second time the lady does the *Pas de Basque* backward and the gent forward—and so alternately.

The music marks the changes.

The Valse attitude is never disengaged. The arms may occasionally be reversed when the waltzers are well practised together.

L' IMPERIALE.

NOAVELLE DANSE PARISIENNE.

Description.

The music is in common time, slow and
well marked.   The gentleman engages the
lady as in other dances, and commences with
the left foot as follows.

1. *Levé.*—*Chassé* (2,)   *Coupé*, (3,)   *jeté*
Devant (4.)   First with one foot then with
the other, making together (8 bars.)   The
gentleman then turns four times on the right
leg, as in the obiliak of the real Mazourka.
These four turns on the same leg make another eight bars as will be seen by the following ;—

Thus, the first step is like the gallop movement, and the Holubiec step is the Sissonne
ensemble, done four times in going round—
or the compass step, [so called,] may be done
in place of the Holubiec turn.

THE TANGO.

The Tango was originally a South American dance, composed in two-fourth time. Arranged for the ball-room, by M. Markowski.

TO BE DANCED IN COUPLES.

Part 1st.—The gentleman and lady at the beginning stand face to face, without taking hands, or holding by the waist.

1. *Echappé* with the right foot, and raise the left foot; the second time to the side, point it down. Spring on the right foot slowly, the three following times quicker. The lady does the same with the gentleman.

2. Give their right hands to each other and place their left on their sides. During these steps they look under and over their arms, which they move in graceful circles four times changing their hands and feet, and finish by *Echappé levé* bringing the foot into the third position. Three *jetés* well marked. They turn their faces from right to left, and from left to right.

The four measures which follow are different from the first, because the dancers turn, sometimes to the right and sometimes to the left. The gentleman holding the lady by the waist as in the tarantular.

Part 2d.—Valse time movements to form the graces.

1. The gentleman takes the lady by the waist as in other dances. He commences with the left foot *Coupé*, bring the left foot back slowly in the third position.

2. A *Jeté* in front.

3. *Fouatté* (whip step) with the left foot, and spring on the right foot.

4. They turn in the Valse, at their pleasure from right to left, or left to right. The gentleman commences with right foot.

The lady does the same all through taking care always to commence with the left foot, if the gentleman commences with his right or the opposite foot to the one he begins with.

LE TANGO VALSE.

A Fancy Ball Room Sketch.

153

HUNGARIAN RIGADOON OR MENUET QUADRILLE OF FIVE FIGURES.

As composed by *Markowski*, of the Imperial Academy of Music, expressly for the French Empress' *Feté*, given at the Tuileries, and as danced by Her Highness and Court Suite.

It is danced in two parallel lines of eight, (or 4 couples,) and may be formed of sixteen, twenty-four, thirty-two, etc., persons, arranged up and down the saloon like a contradance. But eight persons in four opposite couples are requisite for each Quadrille.

Its character and steps are Mazourka.

Figure 1st

1. All join hands—Glissade to the right and back to the left, (4 bars.)

2. Repeat the same figure, omitting the *round de jambe*, and execute in its place the

reverence and salute, (that is, courtsey and bow.) (4 bars.)

3. Each gent with lady by the hand, advance to centre with six *jetés* and pas final, (4 bars.)

4. Change ladies in centre and Holubiec with them by waist, shifting from right to left arms, (4 bars.)

5. Each gent resumes his lady by left hand and to return to places, execute the same six *jetés* and end with *Holubiec* and *pas final* on their places. (4 bars.)

N. B.—These *jetés* are to be made small and kept back and well marked with the music, so as not to advance too rapidly to the centre; or to cover too much ground.

Figure 2.

1. All the gentlemen go to right with right feet and within (viz. the gents move to right in a circle movement, while the ladies move to the left without—moving as a circle movement,) while the ladies to the left, and without, doing a Glissade—Glissade, and *pas final*, and thus all together move around and so back to places—each gent stopping before each second lady, and seizing her in Valse position executes the Holubiec, (16 bars.)

2. Each gentleman takes his lady under the arm, [her left arm under his right arm,] and promenades to centre with *pas Glissade*—Glissade three times, the fourth time the *pas final*, turn to places and return to them with the same step, fourth time all Holubiec on places, [8 bars.]

3. Repeat No. 2, as above, [8 bars.] Bars thirty-two, B.

Figure 3.

1. All to centre *separately*, with *two jetés* and three little rustic steps, *de bourré*, a run with *pas final* in centre—then *Holubiec* in centre and return to places with same steps, 1, 2, and 1, 2, 3, and *pas final* and *Holubiec* again on places, [16 bars.]

2. Waltz by all acrosss and back to places, so as to occupy 16 bars.

Step.—Glissade and hop lightly on the same foot, and repeat with the same foot, making 1, 2, 3, 4. Then walking steps around, 1, 2, 3, 4, at the fourth time, hopping on this foot, or *pas final*, according to the measure of the music, so as not to recommence the Glissade until this fourth time is well out.

Note.

This Valse movement is very pretty, and makes an excellent Waltz in couples.

158 FASHIONABLE DANCER'S CASKET.

Figure 4.

1. Solo by four ladies to centre, with *jeté*
by right foot, left foot before [*i. e. pas de
Basque,*] and two small *fouettes* in the air,
[whip step,] making three times, and the
fourth time *pas final*, returning to places
with same step, having made a Holubiec in
centre in two couples, [16 bars.]

2. All to centre by hand—Glissade—Glissade, and *pas final*, and form two rings in
centre of four each, [4 bars.]

3. Rings around to right and left, [8 bars.]

4. All to places with Glissade, and Holubiec
on places, [4 bars.]—[32 bars.]

Figure 5.

1. *Kolo.*—Viz.: A ring by all to right with
Glissade—Glissade, and *pas final* at each two
bars, [8 bars.]

2. Back to left, [8 bars.]

3. Ring broken—all the gents to right, and
ladies to left, making a circle in going round,
as described in figure second, No. 1. [16 bars.]

4. All Waltz as in figure three, [16 bars.]
—[48 bars.]

N. B.—Professor Markowski, causes the *Reverence* and *Salute*—[that is, the bow and courtesy,] to be done in the first figure, first part, as also in the other figures, instead of the *pas final*, 1, 2, 3, and the *Rond de Jambe*.

Also his *Jetés* are each followed by a slight hop on the same foot—thus giving time to keep the measure. The little hop must be carefully executed.

The following explanation is necessary to a proper understanding of the last figure—as taught by the composer, and with which Mr. F. Troubat, who now resides in Paris, had the goodness to furnish me.

"In the last figure after the round or general ring, and the starting to right by the gentlemen and ladies separately. The eight dancers take hands in a straight line, and advance with a *Pas Marché*, two measures—*Holubiec* in couples in a straight line, two measures—resume hands and advance, two measures—*Holubiec* again, two measures—and so twice more being eight measures, or bars. Then attack the Waltz."

"Markowski's *Holubiec* is a single *Pas Marché* around, and not the difficult whirl, called *Tour-sur-Place*, as in the Mazourka Quadrille."

This dance is almost entirely executed in the Valse, side and forward movements, and

Holubiecs with the *Pas Marché* step. The Mazourka steps used in it, are hardly more than a graceful walking movement, and depend upon *manner* altogether.

The form and figure of the Mazourka Quadrille, are being dropt—or, not now used. It is simply danced in fashionable circles, in couples as the other Valses, and the figures *improvised* as they progress around; or, as fancy may dictate. Intricate Quadrille figures have been abandoned in society.

THE TRIPLET.

A new dance comprising the Gallop, Valse A Deux Temps and Polka.

AS DANCED AT LONDON AND LIVERPOOL.

It is a lively medley—and very popular in the Englisn ball-rooms.

The object of this dance is to combine, and reduce to order, the three dances now so popular. And while retaining all their animation and vivacity, to prevent the present crowding, confusion, and collisions, so generally complained of.

The Triplet Figures—Gallop.

Four couples stand as for a set of Quadrilles. (8 bars before beginning.)

1st. Figure.—The four couples Gallop with four steps into the couples place and turn half round, the same round to places, (8 bars.)

2*d. Figure.*—The first couple Gallop a one with four steps toward each couples place all round, (8 bars.) The second, third, and fourth couples do the same, (24 bars.)

3*d. Figure.*—The four couples advance with four slow setting steps to the centre and gal lop round to left, to places, (8 bars.)

4*th. Figure.*—The first figure repeated.

5*th. Figure.*—The first couple gallop between the opposite couple and return outside, (*a Tiroir.*)

The side couples the same; this repeated (32 bars.)

6*th. Figure.*—The third figure repeated.

7*th. Figure.*—The first figure repeated.

8*th. Figure.*—The first couple do the Valse Gallop round the centre of set, (8 bars.)

The second, third and fourth couples do the same, [24 bars.]

9*th. Figure.*—The third figure repeated.

10*th. Figure.*—The first figure to finish.

VALSE A' DEUX TEMPS.

[The first part of tune is played before beginning.]

The first couple Valse round second, third and fourth couples, and then round outside of set to places, [32 bars.]

The other couples do the same, [96 bars.]

POLKA.

[The first part is played once before beginning, and then as written.]

1st *Figure.*—The four couples set with two steps, and then Waltz with two steps into next couples places, this is done four times round to places, [16 bars.]

2d. *Figure.*—The first and third couples advance and retire, [with one Waltz step and one setting step,] and waltz with four steps into each others places, advance and retire, and waltz round to their own places, [16 bars.]

The side couples the same.

3d. Figure.—The first figure repeated.

4th. Figure.—The first gentleman advances (his partner retiring) with four steps and reverse waltz, 4 steps to places, (8 bars.)

Second, third and fourth couples do the same.

5th. Figure.—The first figure repeated.

6th. Figure.—The first and third couples waltz into each others places, and reverse, waltz round to their own, (8 bars.)

Side couples the same. This is repeated, (16 bars.)

7th. Figure.—The first figure to finish.

Note.

A Schottische Valse and figure, may be done instead of the *Deux Temps.*

☞ We are indebted to Messrs. F. and R. Troubat, for the introduction of many of the preceding Valses, by whom they were brought from Paris, to this city.

MINUET DE LA COUR.

Description and Choregraphy of the Menuet De La Cour.

Explanation of the signs :—Gentleman ◆.
Lady ◆. Give hands . . . . . .   Figures — -
- - - - -

1. One bar rest for the gentleman to take
off his hat.

2. One bar to prepare, and two bars to perform the bow of the gentleman and the curtsey
of the lady.

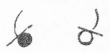

3. One waltz step in going forward, and in turning half around to face each other one bar.

4. One bar while preparing for the bow and curtsey and two bars while performing them.

5. Return to places in giving hands with *Pas de Bourré* forward. *Coupé* backward, the gentleman brings the left foot behind, the lady the right foot forward, two bars, (after this the lady and gentleman always dance with the same foot.)

6. *Pas Grave* forward, in giving the hands, two bars.

7. *Coupé* forward, *Coupé* backwards, in facing each *jeté* to the right. *Pas de Bourré* behind and before. *Coupé* backwards and bring the left foot behind—four bars.

8 *Pas Grave* forward, and *Pas de Menuet* forward in turning—four bars.

9. Two *Pas de Menuet* to the right in passing before one another—four bars.

10. One waltz step. *Coupé* backwards—two bars. The gentleman resumes his hat.

11. *Pas de Bourré* forward and *assemblé* before, two bars.

12. *Coupé* backwards, and two *battements*, repeating it four times in going backwards—four bars.

13. Bend and rise twice.   *Sissonne* with
the left foot.   *Coupé* backwards and bring the
right foot forward—four bars.

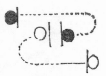

14. *Pas Grave* [to present the right hand.]
Pas de Bourré forward.   *Assemblé* before and
place the right foot at the right—four bars.

15. Two waltz steps. *Pas de Bourré* forwards ; *Coupé* backwards, and place the right foot behind—four bars.

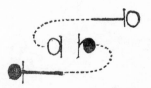

16. *Pas Grave* [to present the left hand.] *Pas de Bourré* forwards, *Assemblé* before, and place the left foot to the left—four bars.

17. Two Waltz steps. *Pas de Bourré* forwards, *Coupé* backwards, and place the left foot behind—four bars.

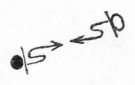

8. *Coupé* forward.   *Coupé* backward. *Pas de Bourré* forward, *Assemblé soutenu*, left foot before—four bars.

19. Minuet step to the right—two bars.

20. Minuet step to the left—two bars.

21. *Pas de Bourré* behind and before, one half round. *Pas de Bourré* behind and before half round. *Pas de Bourré* behind and before, [done quickly.]

Rise and turn on the toes, to bring the left foot forward, and change the feet—four bars.

22. *Coupé* forward, and *Assemblé* before, in bringing alternately one and the other shoul-

der forward. Repeat this three times. *Pas de Bourré* behind and before. Slide the left foot to the left. Finishing with the left toe pointed behind—four bars.

23. Pirouette on both feet, finishing with the left foot behind—four bars.

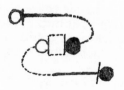

24. *Pas Grave*, [to present both hands,] *Pas de Bourré* forward. *Assemblé* before in facing each other. Turn half round in keep-

ing the left hand of the lady. Place the left foot to the left for the gentleman, and the right foot to the right for the lady—two bars.

25. *Coupé* forwards, *Coupé* backwards— two bars.

26. Give both hands to each other. *Pas de Bourré* before and behind. *Coupé* backwards and place the left foot behind for the gentleman, and right foot before for the lady —two bars.

Repeat the figures, 1, 2, 3, 4, and 5, to conclude.

FIGURES.

SERIOUS FAMILY POLKA.

Composed by Mon. Frederick, of Burton's Theatre, N. Y.

THE DANCERS ARE PLACED AS IN A COTILLION.

Figure 1.

Top and opposite couples dance to the right with heel and toe step, and chassez [4 bars.]

Top and opposite couples take each others places with the same step, [4 bars,] and turn partners, [4 bars,] while the side couples do the same to their own places.

Figure 2.

Four ladies slide and hop, [4 bars,] joining right hands and turning half round, turn opposite gentleman with left hand to heel and toe step and chassez, [4 bars.]

The four gentlemen repeat the whole of this figure, which is danced four times through, bringing all to places.

Figure 3.

Each lady dances to the gentleman on her right, heel and toe and chassez, [4 bars,] and moves with him to the next couple's place on the right, with slide and hop, [4 bars.]

Repeat this to places.

Figure 4.

Top and opposite couples Schottische to each other's places, [4 bars,] advance four, and change ladies, [4 bars.]

Side couples do the same, repeat to places.

Figure 5.

Promenade heel and toe and chassez to places, [16 bars.]

THE EUROPEAN MAZOURKA QUADRILLES.

As introduced by Cellarius and E. Coulan, at Paris and London.

DESCRIPTION OF THE FIVE FIGURES.

Introduction.

Wait eight bars—[take hands round.]
Grand round all to the left, four steps, to the right four steps, (8 bars.)
Petit tour,* forward and backward, (8 bars.)

First Figure.

Right and left, or (*Chain Anglaise*)—(8 bars.)
Top and bottom couples advance, then the two ladies cross over, whilst the two gentlemen execute a quick turn, in giving each

* *Petit tour* is the same figure which was called *Holubiec.*

other the left arms by the elbows, and finishing back to places, (four bars.)

Petit tour backward with the opposite lady, (4 bars.)

Right and left, (8 bars.)

Advance, the two ladies cross over, whilst the gentlemen execute a quick turn in giving each other right arms, (4 bars.)

Petit tour forward, [4 bars.]

Side couples repeat the same figure [which takes 32 bars.]

Second Figure.

Eight bars rest.   Top and bottom gentlemen give right hands to their partners, then they advance and retire, [8 bars.]

Cross over by the left, [4 bars.]

Petit tour forward, [4 bars.]

Ditto to places.

Side couples repeat the same figure, which takes [32 bars.]

Third Figure.

Eight bars rest.   Top and opposite ladies cross over, [4 bars,] and re-cross in giving the left hand, they stop in centre of the Cotillion.

The gentlemen [their partners,] give them their right hands, and place the left around their waists, [4 bars.]

In this position, and without the ladies quitting each other's left hand, they make a half turn, to change places, [4 bars.]

Petit tour backward, [4 bars.]

Hands across or [*moulinet*] one round, [6 bars.]

Retire by taking partners hands, [2 bars.]

Same figure to places, without the hands across the second time.

Side couples repeat the same figure, which takes [40 bars.]

Fourth Figure.

Eight bars rest.   Top gentleman gives his right hand to his partner, then they advance and retire, [8 bars.]   A *Promenade*.

Petit tour forward and backward, [a reverse,] [8 bars.]

The Graces.—They advance again, the gentleman turns half round without quitting his partner's hand, and gives his left hand to the opposite lady, the two ladies join hands behind the gentlemen, [4 bars.]

Advance and retire by three in this position, [4 bars.]

The gentleman stoops and passes under the ladies' arms, [4 bars.]

One round thus to the left, at the end of which the opposite lady so taken is returned to her place, [4 bars.]

Gentleman then promenades to his place with his lady, [4 bars.]

Petit tour [*sur place,*] [4 bars.]

Same figure for the opposite couple, which takes [40 bars.]

Side couples repeat the same figure which takes [40 bars.]

Fifth Figure.

Eight bars rest. Half right and left, and *petit tour* backward, [8 bars.]

Ditto to places.

Hands four half round—*petit tour* forward, [8 bars.]

Ditto to places.

Right and left, [8 bars.]

Petit tour forward and backward, [8 bars.]

Side couples repeat the same figure which takes [48 bars.]

Finale.

Grand Round all to the left and to the right, (16 bars,) and a *Grand Chaine-plate*—(Right and left all, eight round.)

When the partners meet in places, make the *Tour sur place*, or, Mazourka, turn in place at pleasure, (16 bars.)

Note.

We give E. Coulan's description of this Quadrille. The figures being the same as the Cellarius Mazourka. But the description of the former teacher, being more concise and simple han that of the latter—we adopted it for ou little volume.

This dance, like other fashionable ones, has been modified in its simplicity to suit the taste and capacity of the dancing public to acquire with ease and facility its figures and steps.

It may be either danced in the form of a Cotillion, or, by two couples, without the sides, as the *Quadrille Francais* is often danced, which figures it much resembles.

It takes about ten minutes to dance; new couples can join in it at any time. The steps employed are the Mazourka. The great ob-

jection to the Mazourka Quadrille with us, is
its unusual length.

The Mazourka Cotillion is now but seldom
danced in fashionable society, and, like the
Cellarius Valse, which, since it was first introduced in 1844, has been much altered in
steps and time ; that it is difficult to recognize
its original features ; therefore, it is of little
moment to the social dancer—and its interest
only rests with the profession, as to its merits
or orthodox origin.

The Military Quadrilles are a beautiful set,
which are executed only with walking and
gallopade step.   The figures however are complicated, and would require a lengthened cho-
reographic description to make them in any
way understood.   But they are learned in
two or three lessons.   Our limited volume
precludes their insertion.

THE CELLARIUS WALTZ MAZOURKA.

This has the French Dancing terms, as described by himself.

The Waltz Mazourka is composed of three distinct parts, which are executed at pleasure; I have given to the first part the name *Valse simple;* to the second, that of the *Coup de talon;* and to the third that of *Valse double.*

The dancer places himself before his partner as for the ordinary waltz. The departure is made on the left foot by a *temps-levé* on the side, and gliding to the second position: he then pirouettes by leaping on the left foot, and lifting the right leg to re-commence with that leg. So much for the first part.

The second part is done by the aid of the stroke of the heel, which I have previously explained in the article on the Mazourka.

You extend on the side without turning to re-commence with the other leg. This step is performed by four times on one leg, and four times on the other.

For the third part, you execute the two steps of a departure which I have explained in the first. After the second step, when the left leg is in air, and the dance is on the extremity of the foot, he gives at the expiration of the bar, a stroke of the heel, sharp and well marked, drawing the right leg on the side to recommence with that leg.

The first part of this waltz is executed to the right, left, forward, backward, the same as the Polka.

SCOTCH REEL.

The Scotch Reel is a true national dance, and is at times performed by the nobility before her Majesty at her State balls—from State reasons—it is certainly characteristic of Scotland, whence it emanates. The music is generally played by a piper, at Her Majesty's balls, and is played very fast. When the band plays it instead of a piper, one half-play while the other wait their turn, as the Scotch are indefatigable when dancing the reel; they seem almost intoxicated with it—they snap their fingers—throw their arms and feet in the air—screech out—and make such quick and difficult steps that the eyes have trouble to follow them. The figure is danced by two

Ladies and two Gentlemen forming a line of four, the Ladies in the center. (It is danced by our people, under the name of a straight four, throught out the U. S.) They begin with a chain in passing in and out of each other, (a straight right and left) until the two gentlemen return to places, the ladies finish facing the gentlemen; then they set (or balancé) before each other, the gentlemen exhibiting all their skill, the Ladies dancing as quietly as possible; after 8 bars of this set they begin again the chain and set, and this they do as long as they can—in fact they never seem tired, and seem to acquire fresh strength each time they come to the balancè.

The Editor of this work would beg to remark that the steps used by the Scotch in this Reel, is our Polka Valse step—but, not done of course in waltz position.

BALL DRESS FOR GENTLEMEN.

Taste in dress varies with the seasons as its designs are multiform. But *fashion* has established laws in this respect, from which well bred persons are unwilling to depart, and which polished society inflexibly adheres to. We will venture to suggest a few remarks

upon the subject :—Showy colors should be
avoided ; a black coat is always " in keeping,"
(*a dress coat*, of course—we shudder at the
appearance of a man in a ball-room, wearing
a frock coat.)

Waistcoats may be of satin, silk, or plain
white ; gaudy patterns should be avoided ;
neatness in costume becomes elegance.   Pan-
taloons must be black, japan'd leather boots,
or pumps, and black silk stockings.   Scarf,
petit tie, or neckerchief of plain or figured
silk or satin.   Jewellery may be worn in mo-
deration — the less the better ;) an ostenta-
tious display of chains, rings, and pins, is a
personification of vulgarity.

A white handkerchief, and white or lemon-
colored gloves, will complete a gentlemanly
dress.   Do not forget the hair dressing.   Our
preface from a lady of taste, will be perused,
we hope, with pleasure by our female readers.
Gallantry therefore, forbids that, we should
intrude in any further remarks to the *belle* of
the ball-room ; being convinced of the truth
of the adage :

"Beauty unadorned, is adorned the most."

ETIQUETTE OF THE BALL ROOM.

Invitation to private balls should be issued
a week before hand.   Go to a private ball at
an hour suited to the habits of those that in-

vite you.   It is extremely inconvenient, however, to be too early, as you very much disconcert your friends.   To a public ball, ten o'clock is quite early enough.   This makes such late assemblies, one of the abuses of dancing.   Never present an ungloved hand to a lady.   Do not dance too often with the same lady (unless she be affianced to you.)

You should not intrude yourself on the attention of a lady when the services of a friend, or, the master of the ceremonies, are available for an introduction.   Do not intrude your conversation on any other than your partner *pro tcm*, by doing so you commit a double fault, you slight the lady who has a claim on all your attention, and interfere with the privilege of the gentleman who may be dancing with the party you address.

Avoid all appearance of diffidence or awkwardness, on entering a ball-room.   Modest confidence is the characteristic of a gentleman.   Do not be too familiar even with your intimates.   In offering refreshment, or any other attention to a lady, avoid being urgent. A sensible woman will at once accept or decline, as her inclination suits ; and to be pestered in opposition to her wish, gives offence.

We could enlarge upon this subject, but it is unnecessary, as to those who are in the habit of attending *soirées Dansantes*, the usual etiquette in them, is well understood.

A GLOSSARY OF FRENCH TERMS USED IN DANCING.

Chaine Anglaise—Right and left.

Demie Chaine Anglaise—Half right and left.

Balancez—Set to partners.

Chaine des dames—Ladies' Chain.

Tour des mains—Turn to partners.

Demie Promenade—Half promenade.

En avant deux, or en avant et en arriere—The first lady and opposite gentleman advance and retire.

Chassez à droite et à gauche—Move to the right and left.

Traversez—The two opposite persons exchange places.

Re-traversez—Return to places.

Traversez deux en donnant la main droite—The two opposite exchange places giving right hands.

Re-traversez en donnant la main gauche—The opposite re-cross, giving left hands.

Balancez quatre en ligne—The four dancers set in a line, holding both hands.

Dos à Dos—The two opposite persons pass round each other.

En avant quatre et en arriere—The four opposite persons advance and retire.

En avant trois deux fois—Advance three, twice.

Demie tour à quatre—Four hands left round.

Chasez croisez, tous les huit, et de chasez—Gentlemen all change places with partners, and back again.

Les Dames en Moulinet—Ladies right hands across, half round, and back again with left.

Balancez en Moulinet—The gentlemen join right hands with partners, and set in the form of a cross.

Pas d'Allemande—The gentlemen turn their partners under their arms.

Grande Promenade tous les huit—All the eight dancers promenade.

A la fin—All finish.

Contre partie pour les autres—The other dancers do the same.

Chaine des dames double—Double Ladies' Chain, which is performed by all the ladies commencing at the same time.

Chaine Anglaise double—The right and left double.

Le Grand rond—All join hands and advance and retire twice.

Balancez en rond—All join hands and set in a circle.

La grande tour de rond—All join hands and dance quite round to places.

A vos places—To your places.

Tour à coin—Turn the corners.

Deme Moulinet—The ladies all advance to the centre, giving right hands, and return to places.

La meme pour les cavaliers—The gentlemen do the same.

Pas de Basque—This step is peculiar to Southern France, and bears a strong resemblance to the step of the *Redowa.*

Les Tiroirs.—The top and opposite couples pass through each other, changing places. The ladies pass in the centre and the gentlemen outside of them. The step used may be the *Gallopade*, or, *simply walking.*

The return to places is the same, (8 bars.)

The Grand Square.—The leading couples advance to centre together, at the same time the side couples separate from each other side ways, the ladies to their right corners, the gents to their left corners. They, (the sides,) move into the places of the leading couples—while the leading couples glide into the vacated sides. The sides then move up to centre, while the leading couples separate as the sides did, to reach the corners, and so to their own places, while the sides move by the right and left into their own places.

This figure is effected by four distinct movements for each person—*all* must *move together*—each dancer making a square in one corner of the Cotillion and the whole figure makes the *Grand Square.*

Note.—The Polka Step as spplied by our Dancers, is now being done in Europe.

END.